# WITNESS
## TO HIS
# RETURN

## Personal Encounters with Christ

G. Scott Sparrow

Edited by Mark A. Thurston

Foreword by Raymond Moody

A.R.E. Press • Virginia Beach • Virginia

# Table of Contents

To Hugh Lynn—
a once and future disciple

# Foreword

The experiences called visions are among the most remarkable phenomena of the human mind. But to the average person in our day and age, the very name conjures up something misty and remote and antique. We tend to think of visions as experiences accessible only to a few "gifted" individuals whom we imagine to have a direct line to God, unavailable to most of us. Alternatively, we might tend to think of these experiences as mental aberrations.

It has turned out in the past couple of decades that, in fact, there are hordes of visionaries out there—ordinary, everyday men and women (and children, too) functioning well in all walks of life and not at all mentally ill. And it further turns out that the reason that they weren't talking about their experiences has been because of fear of being labeled "crazy" by others and because they assumed that they were unique: that no one else would understand.

There have been many societies in the history and prehistory of our species in which visionary experience was an everyday occurrence. It was no more unusual, really, than what we—in our insulated, technological, television-watching world—regard as "ordinary waking reality." We actually don't know what our society would be like were we to support (rather than to suppress, as we do) visionary consciousness. It is, however, I believe, time to extend encouragement.

This book is an important step toward such encouragement. The researchers, Scott Sparrow and Mark Thurston, report on and analyze the visionary encounters of ordinary people, and it is a good beginning toward understanding the phenomenon as a whole. The primary focus of this book is visionary experiences in which individuals feel they have encountered Christ. Such meetings with Christ—or often simply labeled a "being of light"—are one of the recurrent patterns in near-death experiences, as many investigators have reported. Although few of the accounts in this book are associated with near-death traumas, there are similarities in the experiences.

In addition to reporting visionary experiences, Sparrow and Thurston have identified the *roles* played by the Christ figure in the accounts they have collected: for example, instigator of healing, awakener of spiritual relationship, comforter in times of testing, instructor of spiritual lessons, and source of guidance for life's decisions. In my own research with near-death experiences, the "being of light" most often played roles such as Socratic questioner, provoker of reflection, director of a life review, and clarifier of a sense of mission. Although the categories are not identical, the themes overlap and support each other. The reader will have to make his or her own decision: Is the being of light in a near-death experience the same one who appears in these visionary encounters of Christ?

This book warrants serious consideration and study as we, as a society, try to make sense for ourselves of the nature of these unusual states of awareness and of their bearing on the spiritual life of humankind.

Raymond Moody, M.D., Ph.D.

# Introduction

In the following chapters, I present a variety of heretofore unreported experiences. These accounts are from individuals who tell of having encountered Christ in visions and dreams. Given the sensitive nature of this subject, I feel that the reader should know something about my background and my interests, both of which have undoubtedly influenced my treatment of the Christ encounters presented here.

I gradually became interested in contemporary encounters with Christ after starting to experience them myself, starting in my mid-20s. After being raised a Methodist and experiencing intense but short-lived religious feelings throughout my early life, I awakened to a sustained sense of spiritual yearning that followed a life-changing experience when I was 19. While I did not encounter a personal Christ in that first experience, His *conspicuous absence* served to awaken me to the possibility of meeting Him face to face.

I had already completed my first semester in college. An old childhood friend of mine, who was also attending the University of Texas, had been trying to get me involved in a spiritual growth-oriented study group ever since I had arrived in Austin. Up to that point, however, I was more interested in dating than in contemplating the mysteries of the universe. Then everything changed.

In a dream I shall never forget, I became aware that I was, in fact, dreaming—totally conscious and in possession of my senses. It was my first "lucid dream," which is the phenomenon of being fully aware that one is dreaming *during* the dream.

As the experience began to unfold, I marveled at the seeming paradox of my full wakefulness while in the dream state. I approached a small chapel-like building. As I opened the large, black double-doors, I was immediately infused with a brilliant white light that also permeated the interior. As I walked around the room, I was overwhelmed by joy and a feeling of being home. I also sensed tremendous purposefulness, but *no one was there to explain to me what was happening*. I wondered why. Even as I was deeply affected by the ecstasy of that experience, there was still something or someone missing. Then I awakened.

I thought it was high time to get involved with the study group after that dream!

The study group revolved around the analysis of dreams, the practice of regular lengthy meditations—up to a total of two hours on some days—and the discussion of such subjects as reincarnation and paranormal experiences. Several of us met daily for meditation in a Catholic church near the campus, and we would often get together at our respective apartments on an impromptu basis. During that time, I got to know my collaborator and editor, Mark Thurston. We shared an apartment during my second year at the University, and we have been close friends ever since.

It was in the fertile environment of this deeply meaningful study group involvement that other luminous dreams and apparent out-of-body experiences began to happen to me. It took lots of reading and feedback from my friends to understand what was happening. Quite simply, the dreams and semi-waking experiences which began to occur involved the activation of an intense electricity-like energy in my body. I later identified this powerful but "friendly" force as the kundalini energy mentioned in Eastern writings—a typically dormant force—associated with the awakening of higher consciousness and spiritual evolution of the individual.

Simultaneously, I would sometimes perceive a bright white light, which typically appeared in my dreamscapes as a UFO or a heavenly body—like the moon or the sun. On occasions when I felt the light infuse me, the experience became ecstatically wonderful and visually radiant. But it was nonetheless hard to endure. It was like having too much of the best thing imaginable.

During the time when I was having many of these white light dreams, I shared some of these experiences with my friend and mentor, Dr. Herbert Puryear. Instead of saying, "Wonderful," he asked, "Why do you settle for that?" I was a bit irritated by his question, but I felt challenged as well. I began to look at how I might have been imposing my own limitations upon a Being who might reveal Itself to me in a more personal way, if I could only allow It. I knew that Herb was deeply committed to Christ and thought that I, too, should take a look at that relationship.

Another event happened around that time. During the holidays of 1972-'73, I met with Hugh Lynn Cayce—the late son of Edgar Cayce—who was at that time president of the Association for Research and Enlightenment. We had been corresponding for about two years, and I made an appointment to see him during a visit to the A.R.E. Headquarters in Virginia Beach. I entered his office on a late December morning to find him sitting in front of his large desk. I don't recall many of the details of that talk; but I do remember that he shared with me some of his encounters with Jesus.

When I walked out of his office, for the next three days I felt—or knew—something I'd never experienced before: I sensed Jesus' tangible presence with me. It was so strong that I didn't even want to go to sleep. I was disappointed when the intensity of the feeling gradually subsided.

Still, I had not yet met Him face to face. As I consciously began to affirm a personal relationship with Him, the white light in the deep dreams became more and more personified. It first appeared as a woman—a beautiful Mary-like figure who simply introduced herself on one occasion, instructed me on a later occasion, and administered healing in a deeply troubling dream on still another occasion. Finally, in the spring of 1975, I had my first light experience in which Jesus appeared.

*I soon realized that all my white light dreams and out-of-body experiences were preparations for the more precious experience of encountering Him.*

As I contemplate that first Christ encounter from the vantage point of writing a book about such experiences with the help of my old friend Mark Thurston, it seems uncanny and yet somehow typical that Mark was present in my first Christ encounter, too! In fact, he essentially pointed the way in that experience.

While in a fully conscious lucid dream/out-of-body experience, I found myself with Mark (who himself later reported no memory of the experience). At one point, I saw him standing in a doorway at the back of an auditorium, talking to someone beyond the threshold. I knew it was Jesus!

Anxiously, I walked through the door and looked toward Him. At first I was only able to see bright white light. But then I could see Him clearly in the midst of the light. He was strikingly handsome and similar to the traditional pictures, except that His hair and beard seemed darker than usually depicted, perhaps because He was surrounded by the bright light.

I stood silent and awed by His presence. I felt great love from Him, but sternness as well. He finally asked me, "Are you ready to leave the earth, yet?" I realized that He was asking if I were ready to die. Startled by the implications of His question, I said, "No." He then said, "Then go out and do what you know to do."

Looking back, I realize that I was wavering at that time in my commitment to the spiritual path. It should come as little surprise to anyone that the dream effectively nudged me back on course! His words still remind me to take stock of the work I am doing and to determine whether or not it serves Him.

After this initial direct encounter, the white light and Jesus became virtually interchangeable in my mind. In recent years, this white light experience has come to me less frequently; but Jesus' presence usually accompanies it.

Like many of the Christ encounter recipients whose experiences are recounted in the following chapters, I didn't have a lifelong, conscious relationship to Christ prior to the onset of these experiences. Except for responding to two altar calls during my childhood and adolescence, I felt little conscious interest in the Jesus promoted by the modern church.

Even though the study group in Austin practiced Christian-oriented forms of meditation and prayer as described by Edgar Cayce, the historic Jesus at that time seemed very unimportant to me. I honestly don't recall thinking much about Him, preferring instead to study the contemplative and mystical orders of several of the great religious traditions, including Christianity. But once the experiences with Jesus started, I began to accept Him as the Master whom I could best serve.

I know that many people who are followers of the Eastern tradition believe that a serious spiritual seeker should have a living or physically incarnate master. Since I have encountered Jesus on several occasions which in intensity and clarity exceeded ordinary waking experiences, I have never felt that my relationship with Him was limited by His presumed nonphysical status. To the contrary, I have often thought— with some amusement—that I have probably seen Him face to face more than I would have seen a living master from the Far East, had I chosen to follow one.

In fact, I have two friends who, because they cannot afford to travel halfway around the world, have never seen their masters face to face, except in dreams. So I guess that they *and* I gain access to our masters in the same way. Indeed, I believe that communing with enlightened beings has very little to do with their physicality or location. Instead, it has everything to do with one's state of mind and heart.

The teachings of Edgar Cayce have been very helpful to my understanding of this matter. In one of his many clairvoyant discourses—called "readings"—pertaining to Jesus, he responded to a question about where Jesus could be found today. Was He in any particular heavenly sphere or was He manifesting on earth in another body? Cayce responded in a way that portrays Christ as ever-present to those who invite His presence through love and action:

. . . all power in heaven, in earth, is given to Him who overcame. Hence He is of Himself in space, in the force that impels through faith, through belief, in the individual entity. As a Spirit Entity. Hence not in a body in the earth, but may come at will to him who *wills* to be one with, and acts in love to make same possible. For, He shall come as ye have seen

Him go, in the *body* He occupied in Galilee. The body that He formed, that was crucified on the cross, that rose from the tomb, that walked by the sea, that appeared to Simon, that appeared to Philip . . . (5749-4)[1]

As I prepared to write about these Christ encounters, I realized that my own experiences represented both a strength and a weakness. While I might appreciate the emotional and spiritual impact of the Christ encounter—and try my best to convey this to the reader—I can hardly claim to be as objective as someone who has never had one.

Fortunately, the literature on spiritual experiences includes a great many works written by individuals who drew principally from their own subjective experiences. One does not have to look very far to find enduring contributions made by individuals who wrote, at least in part, about their own experiences. Paul remains one of the most famous, justifying his calling to be the Apostle to the Gentiles on his conversion experience with the risen Christ. St. Ignatius Loyola, who founded the Society of Jesus (the Jesuits), based his spiritual exercises on what had enabled him to come to know Christ directly during a long dark period of convalescence.[2] Richard Maurice Bucke's 1900 classic, *Cosmic Consciousness*,[3] was spawned by his own illumination, yet he concentrated primarily on writing about the similar experiences of others. From the Eastern tradition, Gopi Krishna's books on the kundalini have been based almost entirely on his own unsettling transformative experiences.[4] And even my own *Lucid Dreaming—Dawning of the Clear Light*,[5] is drawn primarily from my own dreams. In this tradition of using one's own experiences as a springboard for addressing what is perhaps a universally available phenomenon, I have included my own Christ encounters in this book.

Another model that has influenced me in my treatment of Christ encounters is set forth by Raymond Moody in his ground-breaking work on the near-death experience—*Life*

*After Life.*[6] While Moody didn't have a near-death experience himself to provide the impetus for his research, his open-minded enquiry has appealed to countless numbers of individuals who would have otherwise turned away from such a controversial topic. Moody has definitely set the right tone for those of us who aspire to probe respectfully the mysteries of humanity's sacred experiences.

The reader will doubtless come to realize that my own encounters are by no means indicative of any great spiritual development. As a rule, they have been sobering reminders of having neglected my spiritual calling and the need to resolve longstanding problems. From what I can gather, this is typical for others, too: Christ apparently manifests to point out—in the most loving way imaginable—where more growth or healing is needed. One woman, whose several accounts are included in the following chapters, believes that Christ more often comes to those who are, essentially, "remedial students"—not to those who are doing well spiritually. Perhaps those who "believe without seeing" derive their sustenance from their faith rather than from Christ's direct interventions.

Mark and I decided to begin collecting Christ encounter experiences and writing about them after discovering our mutual interest in the subject at a meeting in 1989. Mark had suggested we get together, as we typically do every couple of months. For some reason, I felt beforehand that something important was going to happen during our lunchtime visit. While I rarely have strong premonitions, I said to my wife, Lynn, that I felt Mark was going to suggest that we work on some important project together. I had no idea what it could be.

As we ate lunch together, Mark told me how a woman had come up to talk with him following one of his lectures for the A.R.E. Having known Mark for some time, she apparently felt the liberty to assert that someone needed to write about people who were having experiences with Jesus. She went on to tell him, in no uncertain terms, that he should get to work on it. As he related this experience, I told him excitedly about my false start six months earlier on writing about my own Christ encounters. Given our years of friendship, it took us only a moment to recognize a call to action. By the end of our brief get-together, we had mapped out a rough plan.

We obtained the accounts in this book unsystematically over the next two years. Most of them were sent to us in the form of letters and audiotapes in response to a 1989 article I published in *Venture Inward*, the magazine of the Association for Research and Enlightenment. Other accounts were obtained from audiences at various places in the U.S. and Canada where Mark and I have lectured on the topic of Christ encounters and related subjects. And a few have come from my counseling clients who either experienced Christ encounters before our therapy relationship commenced, or in dreams and visions during the time we worked together. Despite publication deadlines, we continue to receive Christ encounters from people who have heard of our research by word of mouth. Whenever possible, we have sent follow-up questionnaires to each person to obtain additional information about the accounts.

Mark and I originally planned to co-write this book since we shared fully in the original conception of the project. But as we got started, it became clear that one of us needed to be the primary author, and the other a collaborator and editor. Somehow I chose to undertake the writing task, and Mark graciously accepted the supportive role. His feedback and ongoing support has enabled me to keep up the momentum and, I hope, arrive at the right balance between description and speculative analysis.

We have defined a Christ encounter as *any experience in which a person perceives the presence of a being whom he or she identifies as Jesus or Christ.* Admittedly, this definition leaves it entirely up to the witnesses' own impressions. This definition also excludes encounters with other identified or unidentified spiritual beings—experiences which, one can reasonably argue, deserve study as well.

For various reasons, we had to leave out some of the accounts we received. Some were simply too long to summarize, arriving on hourlong audiotapes. Some required extensive background information in order to make sense of what was happening. Others were not clear, leaving the reader unsure as to what really took place.

A few of the stories were quite similar to other accounts. Of course, in a formal research study, all data would have been included or analyzed in some way. But our purpose was to present an introduction to Christ encounters. Consequently, an exhaustive presentation may have clouded the picture of this little-known phenomenon. It is important to note, however, that *we did not exclude accounts because of possibly controversial material.* To the contrary, we felt obligated to include any account that may have shed light on the Christ encounter, even if it might have differed from traditional doctrines.

When soliciting for accounts, we promised each person that we would keep identities confidential. Because we had to refer to them in some way, we decided to retain their initials rather than resort to an impersonal number. So each account is identified by the person's initials. If more than one person had the same initials, we included a number in parentheses after the initials. For example, "R.J. (1)" and "R.J. (2)" represent two separate individuals with the same initials. The absence of a number in parentheses tells the reader that only one person had these initials.

If we included more than one account from the same person, we numbered the accounts in the order they were presented. In other words, "M.H. (2)-Acct. #2" represents the second account for the second person whose initials are

"M.H." It also tells the reader that one other account from "M.H. (2)" appeared earlier in the book and that others may follow. The absence of a second number indicates that a person submitted only one Christ encounter.

I spent months reading and re-reading the accounts before I was able to discern categorical differences among them. I realized that there were at least two ways to categorize the reports. First, I could divide them into groups based on what the witnesses *saw, heard, or otherwise perceived* during the experiences. Second, I could look at the *relationship* between the Christ figure and the witness, and divide the accounts into categories based on what was going on between them. I chose the latter approach, believing that the most important aspect of the Christ encounter is how the experience impacts the witness, not what he or she sees. While there is a great deal of overlap among the categories on which I settled, I believe that the divisions do represent somewhat discrete categories that are useful for purposes of analysis and presentation. They are as follows:

- *Awakening* encounters, which are first-time experiences characterized by Christ introducing Himself to the witness. The person does not, as a rule, expect the encounter and is typically left deeply moved and re-oriented toward life.
- *Physical Healing* experiences, in which an ill person receives healing or an alleviation of suffering during a Christ encounter.
- *Emotional Healing* encounters, in which the witness is healed of depression, fear, and other disabling emotions.
- *Confrontational* encounters, in which the individual is confronted with some as-yet unresolved problem which stands in the way of a closer relationship with Christ.
- *Initiation* experiences, in which the witness is faced with an unresolved problem, but is able to respond in such a way as to remove it during the encounter itself. The experience typically culminates in a full sense of partnership and

communion with Christ.

- *Instructional* encounters, in which Christ issues general or specific instructions to the witnesses regarding their lives.
- *Confirmational* accounts, in which Christ manifests ostensibly to praise, reassure, and express His love for the person without regard to any problem.
- *Forerunner* experiences, in which the possibility of a Christ encounter is intimated, but not experienced directly. The would-be witness may have inadvertently missed or avoided the chance for meeting Him face to face.

I hope that I have presented this material without distorting the truth contained in these accounts. It is my wish that by letting readers know something about me, they can more easily look beyond whatever biases I have unintentionally imposed and see what the Christ encounter means to them. Also, by taking the time to collect accounts from a wide variety of people, I hope that I have compensated for any tendency to derive conclusions merely on the basis of my own experiences. By working closely with Mark—as well as with my wife, Lynn, who has studied and embraced a more orthodox Christian belief system—I hope I have been able to avoid the pitfall of excessive subjectivity.

I also hope that this book will be seen as a step in the right direction toward providing a forum for sharing experiences that heretofore—for various reasons—have been kept secret from the world at large.

Every time I fly in an airplane, a hopelessly primitive part of me believes it's just not possible that something so large can fly. I confess I'm always on the edge of my seat. Similarly, I never get used to the idea that Christ actually comes to us. Each time I read an account, I say to myself, "How can something as weighed down as a human being enter into the presence of Someone so sublime?" I think, if He can choose us, then maybe we can fly, too.

My most recent Christ encounter supports this view that

*we're already closer to Him than we think.*

I dreamed I was sitting in front of my computer, just as I am now. Standing behind me were a man and a woman who were involved in a project with me.

The computer monitor suddenly opened up like a stage curtain to reveal Jesus from the shoulders up, just a few feet away. A soft purple light surrounded Him. He asked me, "Do you love me?" I said, "Yes." Then He asked, "Do we love Mary?" I was puzzled by this, but said, "Yes." He then said, "Then you are My father and My brother." Then the dream ended.

How does it relate to this book? To me, loving Mary has come to mean submitting to the task of giving birth to this project. It has meant temporarily foregoing other activities that I might have been doing for the past two years. I believe that when we submit to such a calling, we allow Him to come into our lives: We father and mother Him. And, in time, by giving Him a place in our lives, we grow to be more like Him. We become His brothers and sisters and, in some sense, partners and "co-creators" with Him.

G. Scott Sparrow
August, 1991

# Chapter One

# Understanding Christ Encounters

The occurrence of Christ encounters raises a surprisingly simple but astounding possibility—that Christ can be experienced as directly and as personally as when He lived on earth 2,000 years ago. Consider, for example, the account of Laura when she was terminally ill in 1940 as an 11-year-old girl.

Laura's doctors were sure that the girl was dying. She, her mother, and her brother had all contracted scarlet fever; but her illness had progressed into spinal meningitis, for which there was no medical treatment at that time. The doctors told her parents they could do nothing and that she would die an excruciating, screaming death. Her parents were advised not to remain with her to witness her last days. Laura remembers her parents and Rev. Lang throwing kisses and waving goodbye to her from the door of her hospital room. Then she remembers a "sea of pain."

Later, after losing her eyesight, she was lying on her right side when she heard a voice behind her say, "Laura, turn over." She said, "No, it hurts too much to move. You come around to this side of the bed." The voice responded, "I promise you it will not hurt—turn over." Turning, she saw Jesus. She remembers no other words Jesus said, yet she knows they talked. She watched His hand reach out and touch her thin, twisted leg.

Sometime later, she remarked to a nurse about what pretty red hair she had. The nurse looked at her in shocked surprise, realizing that the girl had greatly improved and had regained her eyesight. She rushed to get the doctors. Soon the room filled up with doctors asking questions. Laura was a very shy person and there were too many doctors, too many questions. But she could talk to Rev. Lang about what happened: He was the one person in all the world with whom she wasn't too shy to talk, and he listened thoughtfully to her story.

Years later as an adult, she heard that Rev. Lang was preaching nearby and went to hear him. His sermon included the story of a little girl who, as she lay dying, had been healed by Jesus. Today, after two subsequent vivid encounters with Christ, Laura is a proud 62-year-old grandmother.

This first experience was an intensely private encounter in the confines of her own blinded state of approaching death. But to the extent that it can still *inspire us* with the transformative love that she experienced in that moment of healing over 50 years ago, it is relevant to us today. Indeed, her account serves to demonstrate how one person's apparent encounter with Christ can continue to inspire hope—if not actual healing—in others who hear it or read about it.

Of course, it is fair to ask, was Laura's experience what it seemed to be? That is, does Christ really appear to individuals today? This might seem like a preposterous notion. But if one accepts both the possibility of a nonmaterial or spiritual realm and the unparalleled spiritual mastery which Jesus exhibited, it requires little stretch of the imagination to answer, Why not? And if we add to this the modern-day testimonies of a widening circle of credible witnesses, then we might conclude—with some wonder—Yes, He does.

As we approach the end of the twentieth century and the new millennium, there is a resurgence of interest in various prophecies that allegedly pertain to our times. In particular, a great many people—from fundamental Christians to "new age" thinkers—expect the eventual return of Jesus Christ as foretold in the scriptures. There are numerous versions of how this might take place. At one end of the range of possibilities would be exclusively personal and private encounters with Christ. At the other end of the range would be physical appearances to masses of people.

Regardless of what one speculates, many would agree that there is a sense that humanity collectively stands on the verge of either collapse or divinely mediated transformation. Not since the days of the early Church, when the disciples and their followers went about proclaiming Christ's imminent return, have so many people embraced the idea of the Second Coming. Today, the obscure prophecies of the 16th-century monk Nostradamus and the modern psychic predictions of Edgar Cayce combine with other non-scriptural sources to supplement the traditional belief that Christ will soon appear again. Whether personal Christ encounters relate in any way to the Second Coming is a question that many readers of this book will, no doubt, ask themselves.

## A Largely Overlooked Phenomenon

As far as I can tell, contemporary Christ encounters have thus far received virtually no serious attention from theologians, ministers, or psychologists—those who might be expected to recognize their significance. To the contrary, there seems to be a conspicuous absence of any mention of this phenomenon. Even in T.J. Morton's inspiring *Knowing Jesus*,[7] in which the author convincingly develops the proposition that one *can* know Jesus today, only a fleeting and disinterested reference is made to direct encounters with Christ.

Some Christ encounters can be found in the writings of a few contemporary figures who are somewhat outside of mainstream Christianity. For example, Starr Daily, the inspiring author of *Love Can Open Prison Doors,* says that his life as a hardened criminal abruptly ended when Jesus came to him in a dream. After a torturous stint in prison, Daily said he saw in a dream "the Man whom I'd been trying to hate for years, Jesus the Christ." In the dream, Daily encountered Jesus in a garden. Jesus came toward him,

" . . . His lips moving as though in prayer. He stopped near me eventually and stood looking down. I had never seen such love in human eye; I had never felt so utterly enveloped in love. I seemed to know consciously that I had seen and felt something that would influence my life throughout all eternity."[8]

It is interesting that Daily had often dreamed as a child of meeting Jesus in the same garden environment, but had gradually forgotten those experiences. Significantly, Daily follows a largely forgotten age-old Christian tradition in regarding the dream as an acceptable avenue for directly encountering the Christ. Daily went on from this experience to author numerous books on the healing power of faith in Christ.

Edgar Cayce is another well-known figure who apparently experienced several encounters with Christ. Known principally for his clairvoyant readings on the holistic treatment of disease, he is probably the most famous and well-documented psychic of the twentieth century. Operating from a self-induced altered state of consciousness, he provided amazingly accurate diagnoses and treatments to those who came asking for his help. In other nonmedical readings, he addressed a variety of metaphysical and spiritual topics, including meditation, healing, psychic development, and reincarnation. The Association for Research and Enlightenment, Inc., was founded in 1931 to preserve and disseminate his ideas; and several well-known biographies have explored his life and work.

Cayce was a deeply religious Christian and an immensely popular Presbyterian Sunday school teacher. Yet, he never made his Christ encounters a matter of public record. One of the few ways that we know about his experiences is through his private correspondence. For example, he speaks of such an experience in a letter he wrote to a friend in 1939:

"Often I have felt, seen and heard the Master at hand. Just a few days ago I had an experience which I have not even told the folk here. As you say, they are too scary to tell, and we wonder at ourselves when we attempt to put them into words, whether we are to believe our own ears, or if others feel we are exaggerating or drawing on our imagination; but to us indeed they are often that which we feel if we hadn't experienced we could not have gone on.

"This past week I have been quite 'out of the running,' but Wednesday afternoon when going into my little office or den for the 4:45 meditation, as I knelt by my couch I had the following experience: First a light gradually filled the room with a golden glow, that seemed to be very exhilarating, putting me in a buoyant state. I felt as if I were being given a healing. Then, as I was about to give the credit to members of our own group who meet at this hour for meditation (as I felt each and every one of them were praying for and with me), *He* came. He stood before me for a few minutes in all the glory that He must have appeared in to the three on the Mount. Like yourself, I heard the voice of my Jesus say, 'Come unto me and rest.' " (Supplement to reading 281-13)[9]

In addition to his extraordinary faith, Cayce's actual encounters with Christ probably had something to do with sustaining his commitment to a life of serving others. Considering how little time he took for himself during his later years—when his reputation was attracting a never-ending stream of requests for readings—one is left to conclude that he derived the greatest satisfaction and meaning in life from serving the Lord who had appeared to him during his hours of need.

Psychiatrist George Ritchie has reported one of the most detailed Christ encounters in the literature. While his encounter has been thought of as primarily a near-death experience (NDE)—perhaps the most famous NDE on record—it is still, above all, an encounter with Jesus Christ. As we shall see in the following chapters, very little meaningful distinction can be made between near-death Christ encounters and those occurring in non-life-threatening circumstances.

While Ritchie was ill with pneumonia, he was administered a drug to which he reacted so severely that he was pronounced clinically dead and remained so for several minutes prior to his resuscitation. During this interval, Ritchie experienced an encounter with Jesus and, presumably, received a detailed view of the afterlife.

As in so many Christ encounters, when Christ appeared to Ritchie, he realized that:

"This person was power itself, older than time and yet more modern than anyone I'd ever met.

"Above all, with that same mysterious inner certainty, I

knew that this man loved me. Far more even than power, what emanated from this Presence was unconditional love. An astonishing love. A love beyond my wildest imagining. This love knew every unlovable thing about me . . . and accepted and loved me just the same."[10]

One might think that such intense experiences would be the exclusive province of a very few devout individuals. But from what I have discovered in my preliminary research, Christ encounters apparently happen as much to ordinary individuals who are simply striving in their own way to do their best. From a scriptural standpoint, this is what one might expect. We're told in the Gospel of John that Jesus made it clear to His followers that He would manifest Himself to anyone who loved Him and followed His commandments.

Understandably, most of us give this promise little thought. Or if we do, we disqualify ourselves without examining the reasons. Feeling unworthy, we may assume that Christ would manifest only to those who live exceedingly virtuous lives; and that rules most of us out. Or, feeling insignificant in the cosmic scheme of things, we assume that He would manifest Himself only to individuals who have far greater needs than our own. In this vein, one friend of mine, who prayerfully calls upon the assistance of spirit guides and Eastern gurus, told me that she felt Jesus had much more important things to do than to attend to her.

Even if we allowed ourselves to expect such a visitation on the basis of Jesus' promises recorded in the New Testament, what if He did not come? Would that not underscore our sense of unworthiness or feelings of abandonment? Or, maybe worse yet, if He did come, what would He require of us? How many of us are really ready to hear what God wants of us? For these reasons and others, most people find it easier to avoid the whole question of whether or not Christ manifests Himself directly to people today.

## The Problem of Telling Other People

Dr. Samuel Johnson once said, "Wonders are willingly told and willingly heard." Yet, it seems apparent that the act of sharing a Christ encounter is strewn with interpersonal difficulties. When one believes oneself to have encountered Jesus Christ, an intimidating set of problems arises to legislate against sharing this otherwise wondrous experience with others.

Some are afraid that the experience will be seen as corny and all too conventional—part of the allegedly outworn paternalistic religion of the past. Others worry about being seen as inflated with their own sense of importance. Still others refrain from disclosing the details of such encounters because they are afraid of being judged crazy or being called liars of the worst kind. Many of the letters I've received from persons who believe they've had such encounters begin with the words, "I know you won't believe me, but . . . "

There is also the problem of stirring up feelings of inadequacy in other people who have not had such experiences. Even if they share a worldview which allows for such encounters, it is by no means certain that they'll be secure enough in their own spirituality to hear it with an open mind. Jesus Himself admonished His followers on several occasions to "tell no one" (e.g., Matt. 8:4) about what they'd experienced with Him, and His statement about not casting one's pearls before swine is well known. (Matt. 7:6)

Even religious authorities may not be able to hear about Christ encounters with an open mind. One woman told us that she finally worked up her nerve to share her Jesus experience with two different priests. The first listened to what she told him, then resumed talking about altogether unrelated matters, as though he had not even heard her. The second became angry, saying that he had sought such an experience all his life. Who was she, he asked, to have been so blessed by Jesus' presence? As the author of *Mere Christianity*,

C.S. Lewis once said, "Once the layman was anxious to hide the fact that he believed so much less than the vicar; he now tends to hide the fact that he believes so much more."[11]

For these and other reasons, it is not surprising that people generally refrain from divulging such experiences. Unfortunately, their silence creates the misleading impression that Christ encounters are less common than they actually are. Because of this, one of the purposes of this book is to provide a vehicle for sharing that can avoid some of the sticky interpersonal problems cited above. By preserving the anonymity of contributors, the book has provided a way for them to relate their Christ encounters without having to worry about reactions from others.

On the receiving end, the sympathetic reader is perhaps in a much better position to appreciate the experiences without knowing the identity of the other persons or having them present. By reading multiple accounts from anonymous, ordinary individuals, the reader might more easily resist the inclination to conclude that the other person is a better, more virtuous individual who deserves to have such experiences. Relieved of the burden of knowing the other individual's personal foibles, the reader may also be able to appreciate the validity of the account without letting his or her knowledge of the other person get in the way. Thus, except for losing whatever benefits might proceed from a direct person-to-person exchange, a collection of anonymous accounts can, arguably, assist both witnesses and readers in reaping the greatest benefit from Christ encounters.

## How Can We Evaluate the Validity of Christ Encounters?

Given the difficulty, if not presumption, in evaluating any intensely meaningful experience, we must be careful not to impose some arbitrary set of beliefs or doctrines—no matter how widely accepted—upon Christ encounters. Yet, most people would probably agree that an important facet of any investigation into Christ encounters should involve *some kind* of evaluation. For example, just how relevant or valid is a particular experience?

There are precedents that can help us here. Evaluating the validity of spiritual experiences is an age-old concern. In the Old Testament, for instance, Jeremiah struggled to find a way to distinguish between actual communications with God and self-serving delusions. Finding no simple way to make this discrimination, he decided to subject the experience to open scrutiny and test the interpretation of the experience over time. Jesus' own "By the fruits, ye shall know them" (Matt. 7:16) gives us yet another approach which makes the quality of a person's life, rather than the experience itself, the object of evaluation.

Christian concern about the validity of spiritual experiences reached absurd proportions during the days of the Inquisition, when even the most devout individuals came under suspicion. The plight of St. Teresa of Avila is a good example of how attempts to evaluate spiritual experiences have too often mirrored the fears and biases of the evaluators.

Teresa witnessed Jesus' appearance to her on a regular basis. When the local religious authorities—who were threatened by her influence—found out, they called for an investigation. Almost immediately, her life was in danger. Everyone knew she would be burned to death if her experiences were judged demonic. Fortunately, the Jesuits intervened to supervise the investigation and to protect her from the Inquisition.

But even under their watchful eye, Teresa was eventually forced by less kindly church officials to do something totally repugnant to her: She was told to make an obscene gesture to the Lord. "Give it the fig!" the inquisitor demanded. "If it is the devil, he may take it as an expression of your contempt, and if it is the Lord, He will not hold it against you, for you are merely obeying an order which I have given you to protect our holy faith."

With great sadness, she complied. "This business of giving the fig," she related, "caused me the greatest sorrow, for my next vision was one of the suffering Lord."[12] Even so, Christ knew her heart, and He did not abandon her for her compliance.

Eventually, even the dark forces of the Inquisition could not discredit Teresa. One of the most notorious of the inquisitors finally acknowledged the authenticity of her visions. She went on to re-establish the Carmelite order as a beacon of spirituality during a relatively corrupt and materialistic era.

Given the presumption involved in trying to validate conclusively a Christ encounter, I have made little attempt to conduct this sort of evaluation for the reader. Ultimately we each will have to make up our own minds. But on occasion, I raise questions or I point out where a Christ encounter contains possibly controversial or unorthodox content.

## How Do We Know if Christ Encounters Are "Real"?

It is easy to dismiss a Christ encounter—particularly one that happens in a dream—as a purely subjective experience. For these experiences generally fall outside the range of ordinary waking experiences which are comprised, in large part, of external events which can be verified by others. But if one is so inclined, much of our experience in life can be similarly undermined: One can dismiss virtually any private experience, including the mere act of thinking, because there is no way to confirm the independent existence of anything unless it can be viewed by others. Yet whoever takes this position is eventually faced with the absurdity of it. After all, what scientist has seen a black hole or a quark? We forget that science, too, operates on faith and conjecture when it comes to the most profound mysteries of the universe.

Indeed, we would all like to have proof to substantiate the reality of our most precious experiences. But our ability to prove our experiences diminishes as we approach that which potentially holds the greatest meaning for us. Ultimately, perhaps, we are left with only the irrefutable conviction of those who have had certain experiences and the deeply resonating affirmative response of many of those who still have not. Others are free to criticize such claims; but a careful analysis of much of what passes as objective criticism often reveals a defense of simply another form of faith in what cannot be proven. Henry Fielding, author of *Tom Jones*, essentially proclaimed the absurdity of most criticism when he asserted, "Til they [his critics] produce the authorities by which they are designated judges, I shall not plead their jurisdiction."[13] This may seem arrogant, but given the fact that no one possesses the whole truth, it is perhaps the only defensible position.

In spite of the unprovability of something as meaningful as Christ encounters, we can at least confirm their psychological "reality." This is done by establishing that the experience is *widespread*—and that it has *predictable, recurrent qualities*. For instance, Raymond Moody and others have provided compelling evidence of the universality and internal consistency of the near-death experience—to the point where many people believe that experiences at the verge of death point to the certainty of an afterlife. In a similar way, this book may contribute to the acceptance of the Christ encounter as a recurrent phenomenon with predictable features and promote further enquiry into the subject.

## How Christ Encounters Come to Us

The Christ encounters in the following chapters have occurred in a variety of states of mind. About half of the experiences were waking visions. A few occurred when it was unclear whether the person was awake or asleep. In these, the witnesses have typically been lying in bed during the encounter.

One account in the collection was clearly a near-death experience, and a few occurred during surgery when the witnesses were not in any danger of actually dying. In one group experience, in which several persons simultaneously felt His presence, one of the witnesses "channeled" Christ.

The other half of the collection is made up of dream experiences. In most of them, the witness was not aware at the time that he or she was dreaming. A few, however, were lucid dreams or "out-of-body" experiences (OOBEs), in which the witness was fully conscious that his or her body was asleep.

I believe it's important to examine some of our assumptions and biases regarding the states of mind which have given rise to these Christ encounters. Otherwise, we might unfairly overvalue or undervalue an experience merely because of the state of mind in which it took place.

*Dreams.* It is probably true that most of us give waking visions more credence than dreams. We are somehow reassured when people tell us they were on their feet with their eyes wide open when it all happened.

But dreams have not always been awarded such lowly status. Certainly, Joseph's dream of the angel (Matt. 2:13) warning him to flee Herod's soldiers is, all by itself, sufficient proof that dreams can communicate God's will. Countless other dreams in the Old and New Testaments attest to the importance attributed to dreams in the Judeo-Christian tradition.

During the first few centuries of the Christian era, the great spokesmen of the Church typically regarded the dream very highly.[14] Origen asserted that the dream-vision was an important part of God's method of revealing Himself to individuals. He divided dreams into two categories: direct and symbolized experiences. He reported that many of the early Christians were actually converted to the new faith through dreams and visions. For instance, Gregory Thaumaturgus, a major force in the early Church, was converted from his pagan beliefs through his dream of John the Beloved and Mary, the mother of the Lord.

Another early Church Father, Cyprian, claimed to have experienced direct manifestations from God in his dreams. He even had one dream in which a young man of striking appearance informed him of his imminent martyrdom. And, on the eve of his great military victory, Constantine's famous dream of Christ not only accounted for his conversion, but also made a place for Christianity in the Roman Empire—thus ensuring the religion's survival through a torturous time.

Like Origen, many of the early Church Fathers believed that dreams came from different levels of the soul. This approach allowed for the confusing and disturbing nature of many dreams without ruling out the possibility of God speaking through other, clearer dreams. This sophisticated multileveled view of dreams was temporarily forgotten when the Church eventually adopted the brilliant, but arid, rationality of St. Thomas Aquinas. Fortunately, this understanding has been resurrected in the modern work of psychiatrist Carl Jung, who reasserted this multileveled view of dreams. Though an empirical scientist, Jung was compelled to admit that the Divine spoke to us through dreams.

Even so, the belief that dreams are inferior to waking experiences still prevails. To give dreams a fresh chance, we might do well to look at *the extent to which the dream involves the person in a dynamic and rich interaction with Christ and with the thrust of His message.* By looking at it this way, the dream-based Christ encounter may emerge as an experience on an equal footing with waking encounters. In fact, we might even conclude that the capacity of dreams to symbolize complex truths may better serve the purposes of the Christ encounter in many instances.

*Lucid Dreams and Out-of-Body Experiences.* Some Christ encounters in our collection occurred when the witnesses were fully conscious and aware of what was taking place, but nevertheless were in a dream or in a nonphysical realm. The presence of full-waking awareness goes a long way toward satisfying our ordinary concept of what is "real." In other words, when we seem to know where we are, it makes the experience feel more valid.

But since these encounters took place while the witnesses were ostensibly "out" of their bodies, they remain nonphysical experiences—the same as ordinary dreams. Ironically the vividness and strong sense of reality often *exceed* our everyday sensory experience. Happenings of this sort announce their authenticity through amazing clarity and intensity. Almost anyone who has had a lucid dream—whether Christ appeared in it or not—remarks at "how real" it all seemed to be.

Ordinary dreams in general—and lucid dreams and OOBEs in particular—challenge us to ask this question: Just how important is it for us to remain identified with our physical bodies during a Christ encounter? Are such experiences to be dismissed or undervalued simply because we weren't fully in touch with our bodies? If so, then this would disqualify many of the most moving, life-transforming experiences included in this book.

*Near-Death Experiences* (NDEs). One of the Christ encounters in our collection also satisfies the definition of a near-death experience: The witness (K.V.D. in Chapter Two) was pronounced dead, encountered Christ, and was subsequently revived. A couple of other accounts exhibit many of the features of an NDE: a life review, an encounter with Christ, and the message that the time is not yet right for the person to stay with Him. But these experiences did not occur when the person was momentarily dead.

Actually, any NDE *in which Christ appears* can be considered a *category* of the Christ encounter phenomenon. After all, Christ encounters occur in a variety of altered states of consciousness as well as in ordinary waking consciousness. They aren't exclusively associated with physical trauma or any other single mental or bodily condition. So the additional designation of NDE, or dream, or trance should not distract us from the focus of this work. Unless one wishes to rule out drug-induced experiences (as we have done to the best of our knowledge in this study), the particular *state* in which the Christ encounter occurs should remain secondary in importance to the larger question of whether the *content* of the experience satisfies the definition of a Christ encounter— an experience in which one perceives oneself coming face to face with Christ or with a Christ-like figure.

*Channeling.* One experience in particular (C.D. in Chapter Eight) raises an important question about the legitimacy of channeling as an avenue to Christ. Here we find the claim that Christ Himself is speaking aloud to the world through the individual's own body and voice box. There is considerable controversy surrounding the phenomenon of channeling— whether involving messages from Jesus or any other spiritual being. We need to think carefully about whether channeling should be considered a valid approach to Christ encounters.

There is a significant difference between channeling Christ and reporting a Christ encounter that has already taken place. *Channeling implies that the information arrives in an undistorted form.* The person begins talking, and the witnesses are essentially asked to overlook the possibility that the channel could be distorting or making up the communication. In contrast, most of us *assume without questioning* that when a person recalls a dream or a previous waking encounter that he or she is reconstructing an inexact replica of the actual subjective experience. It goes without saying that memories are, by definition, inexact and subject to various influences.

The presumption that channeling produces undistorted

communication with God accounts for the historic controversy—remembered as the Montanist heresy—that arose in the second century.[15] Around 180 A.D., a man named Montanus claimed that Christ was speaking directly through him and two women, providing new information about the fulfillment of the messianic prophecy. He and his associates regularly went into a trance state and channeled pronouncements about the imminent return of Jesus and the creation of the New Jerusalem. Montanus announced that this New Jerusalem would appear in his native province of Phrygia in Asia Minor. Others probably saw this as transparently self-serving.

The Church authorities struggled over whether to declare the Montanist prophecies valid. Their reservations were twofold. On the one hand, it would have created a precedent, allowing the possibility that many others would come forth with prophetic claims. Consequently, the authority of the emerging Church would undergo periodic challenges from individuals who claimed to channel Christ Himself. This objection applied to any revelation, whether it was derived from a vision, a dream, or from channeling.

On the other hand, the whole notion of direct channeling was irksome to the non-Montanists. Never before had anyone delivered God's pronouncements in this way. Previously, the Old Testament prophets had all heard God speak to them and then they interpreted what they'd heard. This two-step process allowed for human error; that is, the possibility that the prophet might misconstrue what he had heard. Channeling, however, seemed utterly presumptuous; for it appeared to deliver the prophecies uncontaminated by the prophet.

For both reasons, the Church rejected the Montanists. Since then, Christianity has typically frowned on *any* evidence—whether derived from channeling or from any other source—that Christ makes good on His promise to manifest Himself to those who serve Him.

So we can see that Christ encounters in general, and channeling in particular, reactivate the age-old question about the place of revelation in the Christian tradition.

What do these various states of mind have in common? Perhaps they all assist the individual to surrender a limited ego-based and body-based identity. This surrender can occur in at least two ways. One is involuntary, such as during physical or emotional crises. The other is through the intentional spiritual practices of prayer and meditation. Either way, it seems as though the Christ-encounter witnesses all report arriving at a state of openness and surrender prior to the manifestation of the Christ. In The Revelation, Jesus said to John, "I stand at the door and knock," (Rev. 3:20) implying that He is always waiting for us to do our part. And what is that? It may be that all of our efforts to bring Christ into our lives end—and finally succeed—by our simply surrendering to a relationship with Him.

## The Positive Impact of Sharing Christ Encounters

As we'll discover in the following chapters, not all Christ encounters are equally dramatic or convincing. Some of them seem to be the clear manifestation of a higher Being. Others seem to be more a mixture of spiritual intervention and personal psychological issues. Yet, they almost always appear to represent a pivotal moment in life. They come when guidance or healing seems desperately needed. Or they come as a call from Christ to serve Him in some way. Of course, it's not always clear what specific need the encounter has served nor exactly what has taken place.

Some Christ encounters are so moving that when they are related, they awaken *in the listener* a profound sense of love, self-acceptance, and forgiveness. These experiences seem to speak to a depth in the human psyche which transcends religious and interpersonal differences. If so, we owe it to ourselves to consider the sharing of these accounts as a form of therapeutic experience. Further, there is evidence to suggest that sharing Christ encounters can open up the listener to having his or her own such experience.

For example, when this book was still in the early stages, I was working with a young man who had derived a great deal of strength from his relationship to Christ. He and I decided early on that it would be therapeutic for us to discuss openly our mutual commitment to Jesus. As we confronted his rather intractable drug addiction problem, we would often talk about Jesus' love for His unruly disciples, and His forgiveness for their weaknesses.

During our work together, I often had the occasion to share some of the Christ encounters we'd been collecting for this book. One day, when he was feeling particularly despondent, we again began talking about people who had experienced Christ's intervention in their lives, including Bill Wilson, the founder of Alcoholics Anonymous.

My client expressed a hope that he, too, might be blessed with spiritual healing, since all other remedies had failed. Specifically, he hoped that Jesus would come to him to help him end his longstanding problem. He had always been able to relate to Jesus as a person and had even written some moving poetry and prose about Him, but he had never experienced a direct encounter.

As he talked on about his desire for such an intervention, I sat thinking about a woman who had experienced Jesus actually coming to her bedside while she had been praying one night (M.L.P.-Acct. #1 in Chapter Two). In that experience, she had reached up and actually felt His hair, confirming that He was, indeed, present. As I imagined that experience happening to her, I began hoping that the man's yearnings might be answered in a similar fashion. I am sure that my own inability to help my client overcome his problem fueled my hopes.

Suddenly, I felt "struck" by a wave of energy coming from my left. It felt immediately familiar. I knew from past experiences in deep dreams that it had to do with the coming of white light or Christ Himself. I continued to sit in silence, looking at and listening to my client as usual, not knowing where this was going to go. After a few moments, my client stopped talking in mid-sentence, looked in the direction from which I had felt the wave of energy come, and then said something like, "What's happening? Something's happening here."

Just then a second wave hit and I felt myself almost overwhelmed by it—as if I were becoming very small and surrounded by someone dwarfing me with power and love. I was afraid and simultaneously frustrated by this fear. I suggested to my client that we close our eyes and be still. As we did, I saw white light well up in my visual field.

Later on when we talked about the incident, we discovered that we had both felt a palpable sense of Jesus' presence with us. But, as far as I can see, there was no instantaneous healing for my client. Nevertheless, the event has fortified the man in his commitment to overcome the problem, and his progress toward that goal is clearly evident at the time of this writing.

For myself, this event convinced me that the Christ encounter could be an imminent possibility in my counseling work as well as in the more familiar, private confines of my deep dreams. This new possibility seems especially probable if my client and I share an interest and willingness to discuss such experiences as a way to encourage His coming.

But this sort of openness and encouragement doesn't guarantee an experience. In fact, many of us would doubtless be disappointed even if we systematically set about to experience a Christ encounter. For reasons unknown to us at the present time, such experiences are still apparently hard to come by. Consequently, we should be willing to derive whatever meaning we can from the accounts of others, rather than to make such happenings a criterion of spiritual achievement or the basis of our self-worth.

There is ample precedent for this approach. The history of Christianity reveals a willingness among Christians to study and derive sustenance from the experiences of others, rather than to feel disenfranchised in the face of their apparent good fortune. Indeed, the whole historic foundation of Christianity is based on Jesus' interactions with a relatively small group of followers and critics. Today, modern Christians derive their knowledge of Christ to a large extent from the record of encounters with Him thousands of years ago. Each parable, each individual gesture of love, and each healing miracle combine to form a cohesive testament to what He was and still is to all people—even though He had direct contact with only a few.

Similarly, if we can accept the stories of the people whose experiences with Christ are recounted in the following pages, we have a similar opportunity to derive hope from what is apparently happening in the lives of at least some individuals today. The mere fact that these momentous encounters occur at all might go a long way to deepen our commitment to living according to higher ideals—perhaps also to enhance our readiness to have such an encounter ourselves.

# Chapter Two

# Awakening to a
# Relationship
# with Christ

Few of us expect to meet Christ face to face during our lifetimes. For various reasons, we assume that such events just don't happen to ordinary people. Many staunch Christians seem to forget that Jesus promised to manifest Himself to His followers after His death. (See John 14:15-26.)

Even though fundamental Christians, in particular, believe in a literal interpretation of the scriptures, few people talk openly about the possibility of encountering Christ in a direct, person-to-person way. Of course, Jesus' own recorded words are open to interpretation in this regard: First He says that He will pray to the Father to send "another Comforter

...even the Spirit of Truth." But then He says *He* will manifest Himself to those who keep His commandments. But for various reasons, the spiritual seeker of today—whether steeped in conventional doctrine or otherwise—rarely anticipates such an experience.

The individuals who contributed their stories to this book were generally people involved in spiritual seeking at the time of their remarkable experience. However, they were still surprised when Christ Himself appeared. Since few of us expect Christ to manifest to us in a personified form, an individual's first such encounter is usually quite astonishing. In these initial meetings—which I have called *Awakening* experiences—Christ's manifestation seems to revolve around a singular aim: *making the witness conscious of His living presence.*

As one might expect, the impact was considerable: It established Christ as a personal, caring presence who makes direct communication. Consequently, the experience often signals the beginning of a new phase in a person's life. It's characterized by a commitment to an ongoing one-on-one relationship with Christ.

The following dream of J.W. beautifully introduces the *Awakening* Christ encounter. It's brief, surprising, and enigmatic.

> In my dream, I am walking to a lecture at Asilomar, and I am tapped on the shoulder by someone calling my name. When I turn around, I am surprised to see a middle-aged man I don't know, and I wonder how he knows me. He is tall and lean, dressed in modern casual clothes, and has graying dark blond hair and well-trimmed beard. Although he's quite average looking, his blue eyes are very loving and powerful. He says, "You are a skeptic, J., who does not believe in the Second Coming of Jesus in the flesh." Before I respond, he states

in an authoritative voice, "I am the Christ returned." He
then touches the back of my neck, causing me to joyfully
and peacefully float. I have no doubt in my dream that
He is who He says.—*J.W.*

It's remarkable how such brief and seemingly incomplete
experiences like J.W.'s become pivotal, life-changing events.
In a few words and images, a person's worldview can be
irreversibly altered. J.W. is left mystified, but confidently
expectant as her life unfolds thereafter.

The *Awakening* Christ encounter essentially informs the
witness that Christ *is alive* even now, 2,000 years after Jesus'
death. In a brief dream, D.F. faces the shocking truth that both
His life and His crucifixion are, somehow, happening right
now.

> In the dream, I am walking along an old, overgrown
> railway track. There is an elderly, bearded, white-haired
> man in a long robe walking beside me.
>
> We pass some empty warehouses. Suddenly, I am
> standing before an open warehouse door. In the center
> of the warehouse is a huge cross with the figure of Christ
> on it. The head is leaning toward His left shoulder. It
> looks so real that I cry out, "This can't be true. This
> happened 2,000 years ago!"
>
> But the old man says, "It's now—this is happpening
> now." Then suddenly the Figure on the cross turns His
> face toward me and smiles. I am filled with a sense of
> being totally loved and understood.—*D.F.*

D.F. experienced a powerful awakening. The truths
conveyed to her were both sobering and uplifting. Christ had
been "warehoused"—put aside and forgotten—and His
solitary agony was unrelenting. But His love for her stood out
as the central message. In virtually every account in this book,
there is good news and bad news conveyed to the witness.

The former has to do with what He offers to the witness, and the latter has to do with what the witness—or humanity as a whole—has unwittingly done to Him. Yet, in each encounter His love prevails as the greater message to the witness.

The following experience was submitted by a woman who had reservations at first about whether she should share her Christ encounters in this book. In particular, she expressed concern that such accounts might awaken jealousy or a sense of inadequacy in people who have not experienced Christ in such a direct manner. Believing strongly that her own experiences came to fill a need at the time, she wished to avoid implying that Christ comes to those who somehow merit His love. Even so, she eventually decided that the potential benefits of sharing her Christ encounters with others outweighed the drawbacks.

> My first experience was at night. I had been lying in bed praying. I was pulled away from praying by a light in the hallway outside my room. The light seemed to be coming from down the hall, outside my view. As I watched, the light grew brighter. It seemed to be coming down the hall toward my room.
>
> Then I saw Jesus carrying a candelabrum (which I later identified as a menorah) with seven lit candles. He was tall and dressed in a dark blue/purple robe with crescent moons and stars on it. The edge of the garment and the sleeves were trimmed in gold.
>
> He walked into my room, placed the candelabrum on the floor, and knelt to pray by the side of my bed.
>
> I moved my right hand and touched His hair.
>
> I shall never forget the way His hair felt. I was engulfed with His love and the soft glow that He and the candles brought to the room.
>
> After a time (I don't know how long it was actually), He picked up the candelabrum and walked toward the door. As He walked out of the doorway, I said, "How

can I reach You again?"

He turned and smiled. A warm, radiant smile that had an amused turn to it. His eyes danced playfully, lovingly.

"I'm in the phone book," He replied.

He turned and walked away while I found myself wondering how He would be listed in the phone book. How would I find Him? Then I knew that He would be listed under "Emmanuel." When I looked up "Emmanuel" in the dictionary the next day, I discovered that it means "God is present in the world."

*—M.L.P.-Acct. # 1*

It's hard to imagine one's life ever being quite the same after having such a direct encounter with Jesus. While M.L.P. had been committed to Him beforehand, this initial experience leaves little doubt that He, too, had been actively participating in their relationship. It's probably true that Christians are especially inclined to believe that their relationship with God is a two-way street. But in the absence of any evidence that God or Christ initiates this relationship, it's easy for many of us to doubt it at times. We can only hope that our own experiences will, in time, confirm this article of faith.

An interviewer once asked Carl Jung toward the end of his life if he *believed* in God. After a long pause, he answered, "I don't believe. I *know!*"[16] Whether experience can or should ever fully take the place of faith, M.L.P. can say with a greater degree of certitude than ever before: I *know.*

M.L.P.'s hesitancy to share her experiences is by no means unusual. Many of the individuals who submitted their accounts said that they had related them to only one or two persons. The Christ encounter leaves an individual feeling willing to remain silent, in many instances, to protect the sacredness of the experience. The woman who submitted the following extraordinary encounter did so after years of remaining silent.

I had arrived to attend a prayer vigil before evening daily Mass. When I got out of my car in the parking lot of Most Holy Trinity Church, I glanced at the clock and saw that it was close to 4:40 p.m. I knew that the vigil would begin at 4:45. Hurriedly I approached the street corner and crosswalk. Stopping to look both ways for oncoming traffic, I was aware of a sudden dark deadness. I looked up over my left shoulder to see very large clouds forming. The wind blew strongly and I felt a storm approaching soon. I stopped to watch the quick buildup of clouds overtaking the eastern sky.

From behind the greatest dark cloud, which now appeared to me as a thunderhead, emerged the brightest light I've ever experienced. It filled the remainder of the sky and all about me. I felt short of breath. I could not move. I didn't want to miss this!

From out of this light and on top of the stationary "thunderhead" flowed liquid gold, as though it were being poured. It built up and accumulated in height, from which the form of Jesus appeared.

(Words here seem inadequate to describe the experience. I still cry as I recall the whole event again.)

I stood in awe and obedience before Him. His robe was hooded and fell in soft folds about Him. His facial features were not really distinct, but were there vaguely. The bright light and gold engulfed me, also. I stared and waited.

From under His robe, the gold poured out forward and fell toward me and the parking lot, much like lava, slowly curving here and then there. As I watched, mentally I told myself that the Lord has come for me. "I am ready," I uttered softly. I felt such joy, such happiness, such excitement, yet my physical body remained very still. The golden flowing path was now almost to the parking lot and about six to ten feet from where I stood.

I left my body to meet the path. As I did, the gold stopped flowing. I heard the message, "Not now, listen." I stopped and listened intently, suspended.

*"Be in communion with Me."* I could hear and feel His words. They filled every space within me and about me. Still outside myself and full, I watched as the gold "lava" went back upward to Him and all form disappeared. I was back in my body before the Light was gone.

Now my body shook all over. I couldn't settle it down or make it still. I felt confused, and I didn't know if I should go to my car or to prayers. I wanted to shout and jump and dance and cry and laugh with joy all at the same time.

When I entered the church, prayers were in progress. I sat where I usually did, next to Sister Mary Damian, one of the leaders of our Tuesday prayer group. I shook noticeably, fumbling in my prayer book to find the correct prayer. I dropped to my knees in frustration and gratitude. "Damian," as we call her, helped me by sharing her book with me. I was never able to "get it together" before the service ended.

When I shared a piece of my experience with her, Damian said simply, "I know. It is so beautiful." I felt so full, full of love. Other than Sister Damian, I did not tell anyone about my experience for eight years, and then I shared it with my very close, spiritual friend. I felt that it was such a sacred moment that to tell it as I experienced it might lessen its value.

One thing was *most* clear. I needed to be in communion with our Lord and God . . . Increasingly I walked a narrower path, with a knowing which surmounted logical reasoning. Trust increased. Discernment became clearer. Barriers melted. Surprises came. Meditation became more frequent. I realized that being in communion with Him means manifesting His love in fuller ways with others, as well as with myself, than I'd known before.

I pray for that direction and listen for His love in whatever way it may come. Then, I await to know how best to pass that Love on to others. It is a knowing, not a message in words. My attentiveness leads me in several directions.

It is time for me to share this experience.—*M.M. (1)*

Certainly, M.M.'s experience is one of the more dramatic Christ encounters included in this book. One can sense how her devotion had established an opening through which Christ could reach out to her. One can also feel the tremendous love and authority emanating from Him as M.M. shows herself willing to surrender to Him. While her experience fits the criteria of an *Awakening* encounter, it also includes instruction of a global nature. His command to her—to be in communion with Him—leaves so much open-ended. Essentially, He implies, "Do whatever you must do to be in communion with Me." While the *goal* is set by Him, the *methods* are up to her. One might say that this statement captures the essence of Christ's message, whether one looks at Jesus' words in the Gospel record or at other contemporary Christ encounters. Even though He wants our full commitment, He leaves it up to us to decide how to accomplish this singular aim.

Indeed, the *Awakening* encounter in particular seems to leave a great deal unanswered. Christ appears briefly and powerfully, and then leaves the witness to contemplate the meaning of the experience thereafter. Such is the case with the following account of an 80-year-old Presbyterian woman, who at the age of 18 experienced her first encounter with Christ in a dream that seemed more real to her than an ordinary dream.

I was 18 years old and vacationing at Ocean View,

Virginia, with friends in the month of August. The day before I had my vision I noticed a great deal of activity in my solar plexus. Nerve forces were so strong that it made me uncomfortable. I tried to sit down and stand up to try to ease the disturbance, but it did not help.

That night I was sleeping with a girlfriend who was with our party. I went to sleep and during the night I found myself in a huge hall. It was a very beautiful one with beautiful floors and a few white columns. There were hundreds of people there and Jesus stood at the back of the hall. All the people were on their knees on the floor with their arms outstretched and bowing to Him.

I was standing at the back of the hall. When He saw me, He made His way slowly through the crowd, being careful not to step on anyone. He came to where I was standing and stood in front of me. The light and vibration from His presence was so tremendous that I could hardly bear it in a physical sense. He looked into my eyes, then pointed His forefinger at me and said, "You." His facial expression was stern and yet very loving. His eyes were rather a steel blue. They were clear and I would say more of a blue than a gray. He looked at me with a rather stern expression and at the same time there was great love and tenderness there. His countenance expressed tremendous strength of character and personality and great love.

I returned to my bed and it was still night. I experienced great fear and tried to lie closer to my friend for comfort. She did not help me at all and I was alone. I went back to sleep. The next morning I felt great joy and happiness, such as I had never experienced in my 18 years. All day I was radiant.

I have not made my story public, as I felt it was too private and special. I have only told it to about four or five people.—*M.M.W.*

M.M.W. experienced strong conflicting feelings on the heels of her Christ encounter. There was a lot to be thankful for, but a great deal was left unanswered. Why was He so stern, and why did He come to her? Like many of the encounters with Christ included in this book, this experience was both uplifting and unsettling at the same time. To be completely loved is, perhaps, the ultimate experience. But to be totally known can be painful, especially when our eyes are opened to a forgotten past mirrored in the Knower's eyes. When Christ pointed at M.M.W., she grasped both truths at once. But once she fully experienced her fear, joy prevailed. This indicates again that the overall impact of the Christ encounter is to empower and uplift the individual, in spite of the painful awarenesses which necessarily accompany the process.

It's perhaps significant that much later M.M.W. spent three years writing about facets of the spiritual life. While one can't be sure that her work was a direct outgrowth of the impact of her Christ encounter, it does suggest that such experiences catalyze spiritually oriented work.

In a similar vein, a 41-year-old woman feels that she was called by Christ in her first encounter to involve herself in some form of spiritual work. Two years after her initial encounter, she is still trying to define the deep sense of calling that was stirred to life by His appearance.

I was in my bedroom preparing to go to bed when suddenly I saw a Man in the doorway. He was dressed in white biblical-type robes and was surrounded by a golden glow. Even the folds of His robes seemed to reflect this golden light. He did not look like the pictures of Jesus that I've seen so often in churches. I've since decided that this was because I've never been satisfied that this is what Jesus must look like. Instead, He had shoulder-length dark hair and a beard. I could not clearly see His eyes, yet felt that they reflected a gentle nature. Not a word was spoken. When I first saw Him, I was shocked. I told myself my eyes were playing tricks on me, so I closed them tightly and then reopened them. He was still there. Again, I closed my eyes and again He was still there. Suddenly, He was gone.

I thought for sure I was going crazy, so I made an appointment to talk to a psychologist. I did not tell her what happened, just that there were some problems in my family and I wanted to be sure that I had not inherited any predispositions. She said I tested out fine, although I was showing some signs of stress.

*— J.F.-Acct. # 1*

J.F. was left feeling that she had been called by Christ. But to do what? Months after this first encounter, she dreamed of Christ again: She saw Him and a nun standing nearby, waiting for her. (J.F.-Acct. # 2) Again, she was left with no clear direction. It's interesting that so many recipients of Christ encounters are left wondering what to do next. One might conclude that these experiences are as yet unfinished— that additional installments will eventually complete the picture. It might be hard to believe that He would manifest to us only to leave us with more unanswered questions than before. But perhaps that's one purpose of the Christ encounter—to stir the individual to life and to activate an impassioned search for meaning. After all, if Christ provided all the answers, the newly awakened soul might quickly submit again to slumber.

The witness of the following encounter was involved in spiritual studies at the time of her experience. In her dream, she encounters the Christ in the midst of a radiant white light, a phenomenon often associated with such experiences. The encounter is both dramatic and unforgettable, as well as simple and unembellished.

The following dream occurred while I was enrolled in a Bible study course on the book of Daniel:

I dreamed I was standing atop a mountain. I looked skyward and saw a bright golden light. As I stared at it, it turned into the most brilliant white light I have ever seen. In the center of the light I saw the face of Christ appear. After gazing at His face, I saw what looked like comets shooting this way and that. One landed close to where I was standing and burst into flames.

I awoke and it felt as if I were coming out of anesthesia. There is no question in my mind whether or not it was Jesus. You just know. He is the guiding and/or controlling force in my life.—*M.D.*

There is an economy of detail in this experience. Not one word is spoken, and it seems to take place within the span of a few moments. In spite of its brevity, M.D. was deeply impacted from the perceptually vivid and emotionally intense encounter. Like other *Awakening* experiences, this account suggests that the Christ encounter may occur not so much to offer answers or solutions but to *bring into one's awareness* a conscious covenant or partnership with Christ.

If we knew more about each witness, we would probably conclude that most *Awakening* Christ encounters are healing experiences as well, addressing a particular dimension of the individual's unresolved past. The following account comes across as a classic *Awakening* encounter. It does not directly address a problem in need of healing. However, when questioned further, the individual was able to see that the content of the experience was tailor-made to heal the effects of her emotional abuse as a child.

My experience happened in the '60s during a period in which I was seeking.

At the time, I was visiting Yellowstone. I had a dream that I was in my own apartment and there was a knock at the door. I opened the door and Jesus stood there. It was all light. He opened His garment and showed me His heart, which was a bright light. He motioned for me to come closer, and I saw there were two hearts—joined hearts, interlocking. I'm usually shy and very reserved, but I did not feel that way during the experience. When I woke up, I felt wonderful. I found that He really existed.—R.J. (1)

When R.J. was asked about her association to the two hearts, she said, "I think it related to love. I was an unwanted and abused child and had never experienced love. I had to learn love. I believe that one of the hearts was His and one mine." She went on to say that she believed the experience meant for her "to become one with Him and love everybody. It's been over 20 years ago and I remember every detail of that dream."

In the following dream, the appearance of brilliant light serves as a prelude to Christ's personalized manifestation. Innumerable mystics—both Christian and otherwise—have observed the connection between the interior experience of white or golden light with the highest spiritual states. In Raymond Moody's *Life After Life* and other studies of the near-death experience, the Being who appears to the dying person is almost always surrounded by or bathed in white light. Sometimes, the dying person sees only an orb of light which, nonetheless, is felt to be a Being who loves the person in an unconditional way.

While a personalized Christ figure does not emerge in this dream, the experience suggests that Christ's embodied appearance is imminent. The close connection between the light and the incarnated Christ implies that the two are perhaps aspects of the same wondrous truth: Christ is both a radiant consciousness permeating the universe as well as a Person who transcends all of the limits of incarnational experience.

I was out in a field among a large group of people. I heard music from above. I looked up and saw an energy of white pulsing light moving toward the group. We had all been dressed in white. At the same time I realized it, an angel choir sang a beautiful sound, an entrance song, a heavenly piece of music celebrating the return of Jesus the Christ. The music was incredible. The White Light's pulsations truly moved me to believe.—*P.J.M.*

P.J.M.'s dream suggests that the white light might be seen as a prelude to the appearance of a personalized Christ figure. The following experience, submitted by a 33-year-old Canadian man—who was born in India, raised a Hindu, and subsequently became a Christian—concurs with this idea. He saw white light on several occasions before a personalized figure of Christ began to appear to him. Once again, the light seemed to announce to him and prepare him for the Christ figure's appearance.

It was in 1986 that I first began to have visions of a White Light. Every morning as I would wake up, I would see this White Light ... I would feel very calm and relaxed. I would continue to lie on my bed till the Light would disappear. The Light would normally be there for about five minutes or so. The color of the Light was like that of a white cloud covering a full shining moon. Just before the Light disappeared, a big black cross would appear in the Light. I had this experience for about a week.

From then on, many times I have seen a Christ-like figure. The most recent experience has been in a guided meditation conducted during a talk on "The Medicine Wheel" by an American Indian woman. When she guided us to face east, I saw a very pleasant Christ-like figure appear. The figure had the color of a white cloud; however, there was a brighter aura around the head.

The white color throughout the body was contrasted such that I could make out the silhouette of the figure to be that of Christ.—J.P. (1)

Could it be that those persons who come from non-Christian backgrounds are more likely to experience Christ in a less personified form? J.P.'s Hindu origins might have prepared him to see Christ from a more universal or cosmic perspective, rather than anchoring Christ exclusively in the historical Christian story. Similarly, a Jewish woman, who respects all religions as well as her own faith, experienced Christ coming to her on the rays of the morning sun.

I have been meditating for 13 years. Even though I have been born into the Jewish faith and still actively practice Judaism, I am open to all religions and believe in the unity of all people. I also attend the monthly Unity Church meetings because I love singing praises to God. I also write non-denominational devotional hymns myself. I have allowed myself to be open to Jesus' teachings of spreading love and becoming enlightened.

One morning while I was meditating before sunrise, I felt the sun rising in the east, while it began to shine through the window. The sun filled my heart with such warmth that it spread throughout my being. As I was filled with this warmth, I felt Jesus arising from the sun within me and spreading His arms wide. Love spread over me and I heard Him say to me, "I am the Way."

This occurred as an internal experience: My eyes remained closed. It was very real, however; for the warmth and love brought such peace to my being.

What it meant to me, though, might be different than to a Christian. I felt it to be the true essence of Jesus' teachings—that we can all reach the at-one-ment with God, as did Jesus—that Jesus and love and enlightenment merge to become one. I did not feel that I was to become a Christian in practice of ritual religion—but to know that Jesus is that pure love and God is that pure love, and we are all meant to grow to be that pure love and become one with all creation.—*L.W.*

It's perhaps significant that L.W.'s Christ encounter didn't push her in the direction of becoming a Christian. Rather it deepened her conviction about the universality of Jesus' message. Interestingly, L.W. also said later that she experienced the internal presence of Mary, perceiving her to be "the Mother Divine quality of life, the loving mother of the universe." L.W.'s capacity to commune with other enlightened beings has convinced her that "as we all grow in our awareness, these experiences will become more frequent and accepted, as we merge heaven and earth into oneness for all."

Non-Christians may not always encounter a less personal Christ figure. In A.Z.'s experience below, Jesus appeared and identified Himself to the witness. Given his Vedantist upbringing, A.Z. was understandably surprised.

Following my graduation from high school, I had my first "mind-blowing" experience which shook me to the core. I was living in Palo Alto with a number of young men my age while we participated in a sort of live-in encounter group. Needless to say, it was an emotionally intense and stressful time.

One night I had a profoundly numinous dream of my being in a dark, primitive room standing in the shadows against a wall which was lined with black, aboriginal men. In the center of the room was a skylight in the shape of a Christian cross with brilliant sunlight streaming in at an angle from above, creating a brightly lit cross on the dirt floor. I moved toward the light, looked back to where I had been standing, and saw a Madonna-like figure swathed in colorful glowing robes.

I stepped into the light, looked up into it, and suddenly

the whole dream exploded into an ineffable sensation of electrical energy cascading through my whole being, white light as bright as the sun pouring through me, rending what felt like membranes or veils in the process. The face of Jesus appeared just in front of me against the background of bright white light and a voice said, "I am Jesus." I became aware of what felt like my face turning to stone and cracking, and the face in front of me began fracturing.

The whole episode ended just as abruptly as it had begun and I was left in my bed sobbing in fear and quaking uncontrollably for about 15 minutes. I had absolutely no idea of what hit me but it was not of this world, yet it was more real than anything I had ever experienced, and it was indescribably powerful.

Having been raised in a household with a Vedantist father and a spiritually "neutral" mother, I was unprepared to deal with why the image of Jesus, of all people, should come to me in such a profound way.

—A.Z.

In A.Z.'s dream, we can sense just how foreign these happenings can appear when they don't fit into our current beliefs. The experience can literally seem shattering, for everything that we once held to be true is threatened by the overwhelming authority of the encounter. We can't deny the experience, but we can't integrate it either—at least at first. A.Z. will, no doubt, have to deal with Jesus one way or the other—if not to accept His place in his life, then to argue eloquently for His exclusion.

In the following account, the white light again figured prominently at the beginning of one witness's awakening to Christ's presence in her life. The woman—a Catholic—had asked Jesus to be her spirit guide just prior to the experience.

I was raised with a very strict fundamentalist, fire-and-brimstone type of religion. Even when I was a child, some of it didn't seem right to me and I later sought out a more loving church experience. But I did absorb a lot of Bible knowledge.

I went back to college in my 50s, and one year I took a class in "The Bible as Literature" (thought that would be an easy "A"). At the same time, I took a mythology class. One day in my mythology class, something the teacher said about archaeological findings of an ancient culture in the Middle East shook me up, because it didn't jibe with the Bible. As I left class and was walking along, busy with my thoughts, pondering this, all of a sudden a great white light came into my head. I don't know how to describe it, because it didn't come through my eyes. I didn't *see* it, but it was as if a window opened up in my head and there was this bright light. I heard a voice, quite loud—not from my ears but in my head—saying something that has since gotten away from me, because of what followed. It was only a few words, the essence of which was that I should focus or concentrate on God. Then what happened next was that a huge amount of knowledge was revealed to me. It was as if a disk of information was put into a computer. Most of it has gotten away from me also (I've heard this is very common when we are shown or allowed to see something like this). But again the essence was: God is within us—not in churches or biblical interpretations or liturgies or pageantry. All of that is window-dressing. All we need is ourselves and God in us to guide us.

Well, I was so ecstatic and wound up about what I had learned. My first impulse was to run around campus and tell everyone. Then I thought—I've got to write a book and get this all down. Then a great sadness came over me and I realized I couldn't even talk about it. After this enlightenment, I was never the same. I was hot on the path, searching for more enlightenment and spiritual growth.—C.R. *(1)*

C.R.'s radiant experience resembles Paul's initial encounter with the risen Christ in which he heard, but didn't see, the Lord. While she doesn't identify the voice as Christ during the experience, she says that she later came to believe it was He. Regardless, the experience resembles other *Awakening* Christ encounters in that it catalyzed an intense search for greater meaning and understanding.

While the Light phenomenon is also one of the hallmarks of the classic near-death experience, the following NDE featured a very human Jesus without the accompanying radiance. This Christ encounter occurred when a young pregnant Englishwoman contracted tuberculosis and became so ill that she was temporarily declared clinically dead.

Although it happened years ago, the experience is as fresh in my mind as if it were yesterday.

Well, I was in the hospital and very ill, having contracted tuberculosis at work. We had been testing a herd of cattle for the tuberculosis virus, and the pregnant cows came down with the disease. As I was also pregnant, so did I. Subsequently, I became so ill that I was pronounced dead at one point, and had a near-death experience before I was "sent back" to continue my life.

During the experience, I saw lots and lots of steps leading up to a building. I'd gotten about halfway up when I was stopped by a Man. He wore no white robe, nor did He have wings. This Man was so lovely . . . but there was so much sorrow in His face, so much suffering, as if for all of humanity. He also expressed so *very* much love and compassion. I felt He knew all about me and loved me; but He told me I couldn't go any farther, as I still had so much work to do.

This Man wasn't white or black, but He had very bronzed skin as if He'd been living out in the open and had been in the sun a lot. He wore a robe which I would say was homespun or handwoven. (It wasn't until years later that I heard of the handwoven seamless gown that Jesus wore.) He wore sandals that were just soles with a strap over the big toe. He seemed dusty and weary, but so loving. I have now come to feel that what I saw was the real Jesus.

Afterward, I began searching to know and find everything I could about Him—not just what is in the Bible. I was exposed to that as a child and, although I can now read it with a little more understanding, I have been looking for more.

My earth time is coming to an end and apart from missing the family, I am looking toward going back Home. I just hope I can continue to cope with the pain, and not be too much of a burden to others. I have arthritis, angina, arteriosclerosis, and have had seven major operations—one for cancer, which I now feel is coming back . . . As He said, I had work to do; but I now understand He also meant *work on myself!—K.V.D.*

Like so many of the *Awakening*-type encounters, K.V.D.'s experience set her on a course of trying to understand what had happened to her. As she approaches the end of her life, one can see in her acceptant, loving attitude the fruits of a life transformed by His loving presence.

K.V.D.'s account clearly satisfies the definition of a near-death experience (NDE) as well as the definition of a Christ encounter. Similarly, the following experience also bears the earmarks of an NDE. But the witness—a 25-year-old woman—was apparently not under any kind of physical stress.

I had gone to bed one night and was saying my prayers. I don't know if I drifted off to sleep or not.

I was standing in my living room and heard a loud trumpet sounding; the vibrations seemed to fill everything, as though they were making the same sound. There were other people in the room with me and I asked them if they heard the sound; they said, "No." I knew at that moment it was Archangel Michael's trumpet sounding. All of a sudden, my arms went up (without my doing it).

I started rising up through the room, going right through the ceiling and roof of the house. I kept going higher and, as I went up, a white robe came upon me, and all pain and sorrow were left behind. Joy and peace and love came to me. As I looked around, there were other saints rising also. We were all going to this White Light where Jesus was. When I got there, I saw Him and He told me, "It's not time yet. You have to go back. You have to wait." Then I was back in my front room.

I don't know if I was dreaming or maybe having an NDE. But it was wonderful.—*G.K.*

G.K.'s radiant encounter with Jesus strongly indicates that what we have called the near-death experience can occur in non-life-threatening situations. Physical trauma or temporary clinical death apparently is only one way to get there from here. Surrender of our limited body-based ego can be achieved in less life-threatening ways, such as through yoga, meditation, and prayer. But it's likely that few of us reach this state of surrender short of the physical dying process. Facing our own imminent bodily demise seems to be a sufficient, but not necessary, avenue for achieving the opening that He needs to enter our lives.

In the following account, an individual actually *seeks* a personal encounter with Christ without having had one beforehand. I have found that this happening is a rare prelude to a first-time encounter. Why? Just as few persons are willing to expect great wealth or joy when they have known only poverty or sadness, few of us are willing to seek spiritual experiences when our track record indicates they are out of our reach. Moreover, there is no guarantee that we could succeed, even if we gave it our best effort. Consequently, most of us simply avoid this issue, even when we are ostensibly seeking a closer connection with Christ.

I began to desire to truly experience a relationship with Jesus in which He would become real to me personally. One year as Easter approached, I began to pray for such an experience. I had no idea how this might occur—through a feeling or an inner understanding or a voice or a vision.

One night as I was falling asleep, I had what I believe was an out-of-body experience. I seemed to be out of my body and having difficulty getting back in, and I could sense what felt like evil presences surrounding me. I had encountered similar experiences before and would always call on the name of Jesus and be brought back safely into my body. However, this time I called and called before I finally was brought back with what felt like a thud. I was calling the name of Jesus so loudly that when I finally came back into my body, I could hear myself still calling His name.

I lay there flat on my back with my eyes wide open and my heart beating rapidly from the shock of re-entering so suddenly when a face began to form in front of me. It was a man's face and he had shoulder-length hair. However, the face appeared to have no eyes and the nose was slightly enlarged.

I am not sure how long the face remained—perhaps 30 seconds, perhaps longer. I felt that I was looking at the face of Christ. Yet I didn't understand why I could not see His eyes. I remembered the Cayce reading which indicated that Jesus did not really look Semitic, and so I questioned the appearance of the nose.

As I was thinking in my mind that this might truly be the face of the Master, I mentally said the words, "Who are you?" At that point the face began to disappear much in the same way in which it had come.

The next morning when I woke up, I remembered the apostles on the road to Emmaus and how it was at the moment of recognition that Jesus disappeared from their sight.—*J.P. (2)*

Like some of the Christ encounters we've already examined, J.P.'s experience leaves a lot unanswered. While she might have preferred that the face announce itself, its ambiguity accomplishes more than leaving her wondering. Indeed, this dimension of her experience might be essential for various reasons. For one, it stimulates her own inner search for meaning. A more detailed and answer-filled Christ encounter might have pre-empted this search. Also, it's likely that the Christ encounter embodies truths that cannot be expressed as concretely as we'd like. Carl Jung, in particular, noted that spiritual truth is inevitably expressed in terms of a paradox which typically transcends our true-false, overly concrete approach to life. In an effort to preserve the power of paradox, Jung even admitted that he strived for ambiguity in every expression of his own life. It's, therefore, possible that the Christ face remains silent in J.P.'s experience because ambiguity is sometimes more valuable than an obvious answer.

The *Awakening* Christ encounter often contains symbolic content that is surprising to the witness. The fact that the content does not fit a person's expectations supports the notion that Christ encounters typically transcend our conscious assumptions and beliefs. It's as though the experience is constructed from largely unconscious and unacknowledged raw material that, presumably, is particularly suited to our needs. A 57-year-old American salesman, living on the west coast of Mexico, had the following experience, which still mystifies him today. At the time, he was praying every morning and evening for guidance as he felt very insecure in his work and lonely at home.

I live in a one-room bachelor apartment, and at one end of my apartment is the kitchenette area. No more than 15 feet from where I sleep is my gas stove and oven. One night in September 1988 I dreamed that Jesus Christ appeared above my gas stove. He was standing almost six feet tall with a lamb in His arms and looking at it with pure love—at least this is the feeling it gave me when I looked at Him. He had brown hair, rather sharp features, and a beard. He was wearing a beautiful, long, dress-like robe of a pearl-gray color which had an embroidered border of blue. It was heavily embroidered about one inch from the bottom hem and was about three inches in width all around. At the same time I was hearing George Beverly Shea singing with a symphony the song "How Great Thou Art." The whole thing was really fantastic and beautiful.

Now for qualification. I have *never* been a follower of Billy Graham or Shea, they being in my eyes rather common. My faith is Episcopal with a very orthodox Catholic bent and a healthy degree of mysticism. Also I felt that maybe I simply saw a copy of the traditional painting of Jesus with the lamb which has been so widely circulated. But my dream was not like these paintings, as I have investigated several of them and none comes close. Also for some reason which I still don't understand, the blue embroidered border is very important to me and still stands out vividly in my memory.—*J.R.*

J.R.'s experience departs somewhat from his conscious expectations and beliefs, and leaves him surprised and curious about what he has witnessed. Actually, the unexpected dimensions of J.R.'s encounter help to dismiss the possible criticism that he unwittingly concocted it from his imagination. Indeed, the surprising twists that we find in most Christ encounters announce the presence of a distinct intelligence affecting, if not fully shaping, the experience.

The way that the blue hem continues to haunt J.R. speaks to the capacity of symbols to point to spiritual realities that cannot be fully grasped by the logical mind. Again, we can see that the essential power and meaning of the Christ encounter is *served*, not undermined, by the ambiguous and symbolic elements of the experience.

In summary, the *Awakening* Christ encounter resembles and overlaps with other types of Christ experiences.

But how does it differ?

In essence, the *Awakening* exhibits an abruptness. As a first-time encounter, it typically takes the witness by surprise. It conveys the sense that Christ is taking the opportunity to introduce Himself for an apparent purpose: to bring into the individual's conscious awareness a relationship that Christ *already* recognizes.

It's quite possible that we could assign many of these *Awakening* accounts to other categories as well. That is to say, some of these stories might also fit other chapters of this book, if we knew more about the life context in which the experience occurred or more about its impact on the person during the days which followed.

Even so, it's useful to look at the accounts of this chapter as a distinct type of Christ encounter experience for one reason in particular: The individuals felt amazed and astonished. They wondered, Why me? What next? Often they may have initially failed to see the obvious purpose or need behind what came to them.

Their stories make us appreciate just what a surprise Christ encounters can be—how they often come to those who least expect them. This implies, of course, that *any* person who is

not currently expecting a Christ encounter might, in fact, be
on the verge of having one.

# Chapter Three

# Physical Healings

Two thousand years ago Christ made Himself known to people largely through miracles of healing. Some of the most moving passages in the Gospel record—those which instill faith in the reader during the most hopeless times—concern those instances when Jesus relieved the pain, suffering or lifelong disabilities of the people who came to Him for help. Indeed, His willingness to save His friends and acquaintances from death itself shows us just how much He cared to minister to the human, as well as the spiritual, needs of those He encountered.

Many of the accounts we have collected suggest that His healing ministry still continues. The stories in this chapter concern those Christ encounters which occurred when the recipients or their loved ones were facing a physical or medical crisis. Because these experiences involve specific physical conditions and events, they serve to remind us that the Christ encounter can effect changes on all levels of a person's life. Consequently, some readers may find it easier to accept the validity of accounts which do not produce measurable results once he or she sees that Christ encounters, at least in some instances, yield dramatic physical changes.

This chapter, however, does not limit itself to accounts in which medical miracles occurred. Just as often, in the face of health or safety crises, Christ's presence seems to assure individuals that their worries about life-threatening events or ominous medical conditions are unnecessary. As we'll see in these instances, Christ serves as a comforter as well as an agent of direct physical change.

## Physical Illness and Healing

Our first account involves a two-stage process in which the recipient was first apparently healed of a physical condition, then shown the source of the healing in a dramatic waking vision days later. Here is the experience in A.D.'s own words:

I fell down a flight of stairs and was injured so badly that my lower spinal column was in almost continuous distress and pain. I had frequent chiropractic treatments for it. Getting in and out of bed became a careful process. Usually I would be somewhat stiff in the morning getting up. Even so, I rose at 6:30 a.m. for meditation (because it was the least interrupted, quiet time for me) and to prepare breakfast for my husband and children.

This was the pattern of my life for seven years. One evening, my husband chose to stay up to watch a late TV sports review and I went to bed. I had just changed into my nightgown when I sensed a presence standing close beside me on my left, and a (male) voice said, "This night sleep on your stomach, Alice." The voice that spoke my name was as clear and normal as when two persons are in conversation.

I started to protest in a gentle way. "But you know I can't sleep on my stomach!" I said with mock alarm, meaning that my back would become so rigid in the night that I would need help to get out of bed. Yet even as I said this, I obeyed quietly as a child would, and remembered thinking how astonishing that I could do this, and fell into a deep sleep in this manner almost immediately.

Later, in reliving this extraordinary scene in my mind (and I did many times), I recall how amusing it seemed to me—as I was speaking the words—that I would remonstrate with a spiritual being! It still surprises me. The event is recounted here as it happened to illustrate how natural the entire incident seemed.

In the morning, just before actually waking, I distinctly felt the touch of hands massaging, manipulating, and pressing lightly on the lower region of my back. Then I slipped out of bed as though there had never been an injury!

For three full days I was in a silent, prayerful state filled with awe and reverence, consumed with wonder. Whose hands did I feel on my back? Who was it who healed me?

On the third night, I went to bed a little earlier again. As I closed the door, the entire wall facing me disappeared, and where there had been a large window and tall furniture occupying that wall space, there was now a brilliant panel of light. I stood transfixed, gazing at it. In the center was a Figure in full height, with His hands outstretched, palms upward. He was showing me how my back was healed and who had healed me. I say "He" because I knew instinctively it was the voice I had heard earlier, but this time no words were exchanged.

The Figure appeared to be androgynous, neither male nor female, nor were the hands characteristic of either. The face was so luminous I could not make out the features, but the hair was plainly visible. It glistened with soft brown waves and fell to the shoulder. He wore a single white garment with no apparent seams, that reached from the neck to the floor and covered the feet. Full, open sleeves were at the wrist.

He stood like this for several seconds, and then the wall reappeared in the fraction of a moment as inexplicably as it had disappeared moments before. I remained in that state of grace for some time afterward, and even today, more than 30 years later, the event is indelibly etched in my mind and very simple to recall in all its detail.

Since that first remarkable experience, I have received three other instantaneous spiritual healings . . . More than anything else, it has nurtured in me the concept of gratitude.

Of the initial visitation, I have been asked if I thought it was Jesus. I don't know. I'm certain only that it was a Christ-like figure and am content with that.—*A.D.*

The experience of physical healing would have been life-changing all by itself. But then to be shown that the agent of healing was a radiant Being who cared enough to reveal "Himself" to A.D. must have curtailed any tendency to explain away the remarkable change as a coincidence. It is as though the Being appears not just to satisfy A.D.'s curiosity but to leave no doubt in her mind about the Source of her healing.

There are many interesting features to this incident, but one aspect is particularly important to consider. In this account A.D. refrains from identifying the radiant figure as Christ or Jesus during the encounter. She is even content after the experience to let the question of identity remain unanswered.

Throughout our examination of Christ encounters, we'll tackle again and again this question: Who is the figure *really?*

It is interesting that some individuals have experienced Christ in both ways—a very personal Jesus as well as an indistinct Being of Light. For instance, M.L.P—a woman whose particular encounters with Jesus are included elsewhere—also had a healing experience with a Being of Light. Despite His universal appearance, He loved her personally enough to heal her with His tears.

> I was going through a stressful time and had an excruciating headache—so bad, in fact, that I had wrapped my head in my dark cashmere sweater to try to keep out the light which seemed to make my head hurt worse. My face, however, was uncovered. Apparently I had been writhing on the bed, because I wound up lying crosswise on the bed with my head toward the east. The pain was so bad that I felt tears in my eyes. Then I realized that Someone was standing at my head, and when I opened my eyes I saw a "shining Stranger" bathed in light. He was crying and the tears that fell from His eyes were dropping on my eyes, causing tears that I had thought were my own. In a type of out-of-body experience, I felt myself leave my body and turn to face Him. We embraced and together began turning and ascending in a type of dance of mystical union.—*M.L.P.-Acct. # 2*

One gets the sense that the Light Being manifested not only to heal her headache but also to alleviate the emotional conditions that produced it. As such, this account also fits into the category of emotional healing.

It is interesting to note that in A.D.'s Christ encounter, she actually had to *do* something for the healing process to occur. A physical application was necessary. This requirement is reminiscent of Jesus' manner of healing. He would sometimes require supplicants to perform some physical action as their part of the healing process. For example, in John 9:1-11 we find the story of Jesus' healing of a man who was born blind. Jesus mixed His own spittle with soil to make clay. Then He placed the clay over the man's eyes and gave him a task: go and wash off the clay from a specific pool. Only when the man did this was he healed. On another occasion, Jesus told ten lepers that He would heal them. He told them to present themselves to the rabbi so their miraculous healing could be duly acknowledged, according to the Jewish tradition. The healing took place only as they were on their way to see the rabbi.

Of course, we are left to wonder what is going on in this story. Does the specific procedure really affect the healing process directly? Or is a cooperative *spirit* needed to allow higher forces to effect the healing? Perhaps it's significant that A.D. had to be willing to assume a sleeping posture which had previously been painful to her. In essence, Christ required her to make a leap of faith in a very concrete way.

This same pattern can be found in another account, the story of L.B.K., which was referred to in Chapter One. She, too, was asked to do something that had previously been excruciating. Other aspects of her story parallel the most dramatic New Testament examples of Jesus' healing ministry. Consequently, I feel it is important to include L.B.K.'s account here again, along with her additional commentary.

> I am now a grandmother, age 62. For many years I never spoke of my Christ experience. I wish now that I had looked up records so that today I could have the proof nonbelievers seem to need. Somewhere I know there is some proof in hospital and church records, as I was called The Miracle Child.
>
> Today I can't remember the dates. I was eleven years old (in Ohio). My mother, sister, and I had scarlet fever; my own disease went into spinal meningitis.

My parents had lost everything; my father, a carpenter by trade, had been unemployed for a long time. The state of Ohio paid my hospital bills, even flying in a doctor from Chicago. The part of Ohio State University Hospital that I was in was a building apart from the main hospital with a high fence around it. I don't remember going in, but I remember my father carrying me out.

I remember one of the nine times that I was held in a tight ball and told not to move, as a big needle was put into my spine. Later, looking in a mirror, for years I could see and count these nine marks. I remember the horrible pain and my thin, twisted legs.

My parents were told my death would be a terrible, screaming thing; best for them not to see or hear, to go home. I lost my sight and hearing but before that, saw my parents, grandparents, and Rev. John Lang standing in the door of my room, not permitted to come in. The smiles, the thrown kisses, the waving good-bye, I remember all—and then the sea of pain.

Later, after losing my eyesight, I was lying on my right side. I heard a voice behind me say, "Laura, turn over." I said, "No, it hurts too much to move. You come around to this side of the bed." Then the voice said, "I promise you it will not hurt—turn over." Turning, I saw Jesus. I remember no other words Jesus said to me, yet I know we talked. I watched His beautifully shaped hand reach out and touch my leg.

Sometime later, I remember remarking to a nurse about what pretty red hair she had. She looked at me in shocked surprise and rushed from the room. The room soon filled up with doctors asking questions. I was a very shy person and there were too many doctors, too many questions. I had to talk about this to Rev. Lang. He was the one person in all the world I wasn't too shy to talk to.

Rev. Lang listened, asked questions and took many notes. I couldn't see the face of Christ, as it was like looking into a light bulb. But His clothes, the color and material I had never seen—all that I can remember. I was very blonde with very pale skin—the skin of Christ was much darker. The color of a piece of His hair I saw fall on His left shoulder as He reached out His left hand to touch me was a color I had never seen before. Rev. Lang called it auburn.

My parents were told I could not live—I did. I was sitting in a chair and heard I would never walk—I did. They were told I would never have children—I had three.

Years later—I had not seen Rev. Lang for years—I noticed in a local paper he was to speak at a church nearby. My sister and I were late, so we slipped in a side door. Rev. Lang was speaking about a little girl, "a miracle child" he had known, who had seen and was healed by Christ. Here he was telling hundreds of people of the event that had happened to me—what we had talked about long ago. He also said the child had a light about her for days after the visit—something I had not known.

This visit from Christ was never spoken of in my home by my family—I was raised thinking it something about which you did not talk.—*L.B.K.*

L.B.K.'s narrative reverberates with the faith-inspiring force of some of the Gospel stories of healing. Her experience calls to mind the seemingly hopeless case of Jairus' daughter and the plight of Jesus' own friend, Lazarus. For myself, I know that after reading her account dozens of times, I am still deeply moved by what happened to her. I cannot help but feel that her story exerts a similar effect on virtually all who read it.

As we've already noted, the accounts of A.D. (pp. 50-52) and L.B.K. (pp. 54-56) share a common theme: both individuals had to have a cooperative spirit and actually *do* something based on faith. Another parallel between their accounts is the very *appearance* of the Christ figure. For example, both of them saw a Being whose face was light itself. But other than the face, they also saw vivid and detailed aspects of His appearance.

Whereas A.D. and L.B.K. received physical healing *themselves* during their Christ encounter experiences, another woman apparently witnessed Christ healing *someone else:* her mother. This account exemplifies the mediating role that individuals can apparently play through prayer, belief, and love. When K.M.'s experience occurred, she was 25 years old, and her mother was suffering from the advanced stages of cancer.

As a child, I used to collect pictures of Jesus and hide them in a box of "treasures." My favorite was one of Him on the cross. My aunt, who has cerebral palsy, used to walk me to the Methodist church for Sunday school when I was 4, 5, and 6, and outside of that I had no real religious background, but always believed very sincerely that Christ was there if I needed Him.

I elected to be baptized at the age of 12, and my dear aunt was the only person (besides the minister) present. Her faith was her beauty, though outwardly she was not beautiful.

Since both of my parents worked, I was very independent. I was never really "close" to my mother, but loved her dearly, even though I felt that she was very detached from us all and never really wanted me initially—I just "happened" to her. Mom and Dad fought often and not casually, and I was always throwing myself in the middle. Often alcohol was to blame, and on my mother's day off from work, she would get drunk to forget what might have been.

After I had graduated from college and was teaching high school English, my mother had her first cancer operation: a mastectomy. She had had this tumor for over a year without doing anything about it. She had undergone chemotherapy and the prognosis was not good. After a second operation to remove her lymph nodes in the same side, her outlook was dismal. I was determined that I could save her life through prayer and calling on Christ for help.

I prayed desperately for His help and even offered to trade places with her. I would cry myself to sleep praying. One night, I awoke about 3:00 a.m. and sat up in bed. I was in my bed, but my bed and I (and my dear sleeping husband) were in my mother's bedroom where she lay sleeping. I was aware that Christ was in the doorway, as if He hadn't just arrived but had always been there. I was in awe—a part of a dramatic play, like an actor, yet a member of the audience, watching, waiting, holding my breath.

The room grew bigger in size and cleaner as Christ moved toward my mother's bed. The light was so intense—like sun glinting on the crystals of newly fallen snow—that it hurt deep in my eyes to look, and I realized that part of that pain was my grief for my mother. Silently, gracefully, He walked (glided) to her bedside and touched the side of her face. Then He turned and nodded, gazed at me, acknowledged me, and left through the same door. I woke up and it was morning. For the first time, I was at peace knowing that Christ had intervened for my mother and that she would live. I told my mother and father this years later, but somehow I don't feel that they believed its validity. Mom is still alive today.—*K.M.*

This story presents us with a dilemma as we try to

understand what happened. K.M. showed a deep love for her mother, and a willingness to offer herself as a sacrifice for a woman who had given her little in the way of love when she was a child. The problem is evident if we consider the modern-day emphasis on overcoming the effects of living in an alcoholic environment. Children of alcoholics tend to try to keep the peace at a great cost to themselves. They try to win love from someone who, at the time, cannot give it. Modern treatment of "adult children of alcoholics" has focused on differentiating oneself from the family. Using this therapeutic approach, one works through the anger of having been abandoned by the addict and addresses one's own long-neglected needs for nurturance and love.

Perhaps K.M. had completed this work prior to her attempt to intercede on her mother's behalf. On the other hand, it would be easy for a traditional clinician to interpret her attempts as weakness. K.M. seemed to try to glue together a shattered world for her mother rather than admit her own limitations to take care of her mother. K.M. seemed to avoid the affirmation of her own needs.

Yet, this rather clinical assessment is stood on its head by the consequences of K.M.'s loving intercession. That which seems totally unexpected happens—completely beyond what a traditional clinician would anticipate. Obviously, whatever interpersonal problems existed between K.M. and her mother posed an insignificant obstacle to the healing process. This surprising result simply shows how difficult it can be to make an important distinction: What's really the difference between *unhealthy* self-sacrifice on the one hand, and on the other a *transcendent gift* of the highest form—giving one's life for another person?

Another account illustrates how important it might be to refrain from attaching too much significance to the physical outcome of intercessory prayers.

P.G. was a 33-year-old wife and after-school teacher living

in Florida. Her husband was dying of cancer, and she had two experiences with Christ. In the first one, she saw a vision of Him during meditation at her weekly meditation group meeting. The second encounter was even more dramatic: Christ told her that her husband had been healed. But soon thereafter, her husband died!

The second time I saw Jesus was in a vision when my husband was sick in the hospital. He had liver cancer and was in a lot of pain. I was getting into my car one day to go to the place I worked, and with my eyes open I saw a vision of Jesus standing over my husband's hospital bed. He had His arm raised over my husband, as if He were healing him. Then the vision went away. When I got home that night, I called my husband, and he said that his pain had gone away and that he hadn't had to ask for another pain pill. He didn't understand why, so I told him about the vision. I had a feeling that it really helped him to believe, not that he didn't believe before, but I think it really helped him.

That night [as I slept], I heard over and over in my mind that God, Jesus, and I were one; and that I could cure Pedro with God and Jesus. I kept saying to myself, "He's cured, and I can do it." This happened three times, and then I woke up. Also, during this time while I was praying for my husband, I kept hearing Jesus say to me that he was healed and that he would be saved. I assumed this meant physical healing.

I was checking on him every half hour, and for some reason something told me to go upstairs. When I did, I found him dying. I took him in my arms and said, "God loves you, Jesus loves you, and I love you." As soon as I said that, he closed his eyes and that was it. I knew that Jesus was right there ready to help him.

I was shocked when he died. It wasn't until that

moment that I realized Jesus meant spiritual healing.
*—P.G. (1)-Acct. # 2*

If there is a life after death and if we make the transition slowly as some traditions contend, the process of healing and awakening may continue beyond the grave. In support of this idea, P.G. continued to have visions of Jesus assisting Pedro in his adjustment to the afterlife.

> A month after my husband Pedro died, I had the following experience:
> One night during the meditation time of our study group, I saw Pedro and Jesus. Pedro had his eyes closed. He looked like he did the minute he died. Jesus took him in His arms and carried him to a place and was with him. I realized that three days passed before Pedro woke up, was smiling, and was happy just like he used to be. The place was beautiful with Easter flowers, and everything was green. I smelled lily of the valley flowers."
> *—P.G. (1)-Acct. #3*

Even if Christ manifests principally to heal the spirit, not the flesh, we must still contend with the apparent fact that He does not present Himself to everyone in need of spiritual healing. Is there a selection process based on worth or degree of need? Or could it be that such healing is available to all, but that only a few are open to it? John heard Jesus say during his Revelation, "I stand at the door and knock." (Rev. 3:20) He did not say that He would enter our lives unbidden.

In a similar vein, one contemporary spiritual teacher—Da Avabhasa, who was known formerly as Da Free John—suggests that an enlightened being's influence depends upon the individual making himself or herself available to it. He illustrates this idea by likening himself to a light in a room, which shines on anyone who enters. The room is readily available to all, but one has to make the effort to enter. Upon entering, one might say from the ego's perspective, "The light shines on *me*," when, in fact, it is universally accessible and really shines—without exception—on *all* who have entered.

Another answer to the perplexing question of why only some people experience Christ encounters was offered by one woman, M.E., whose accounts are included later in this chapter. In her opinion, these divine initiatives may, in fact, come freely to all of us, but in our preoccupied mind-sets we may fail to notice them. She wrote, while reflecting on this mystery, "I do not know why these experiences happened to me. I wonder if all who practice His Presence have these 'touches' but are not aware or receptive of them."

## Reassurance in a Health Crisis

Not every encounter with Christ promises a miraculous cure that would astound the patient's physician. Instead, the experience may come to bring reassurance that the healing process will be successful, even with the assistance of modern medicine.

For example, D.T. was a 42-year-old woman who worked as a secretary. By her own admission she had an exceptional need for comfort and reassurance as she faced a serious health condition. Fearfully anticipating oral surgery, she perceived Christ coming to her as a comforting presence.

I was told last year by my dentist that I had to have all my teeth removed, and, as I was allergic to all the local anesthesia, the doctors decided to give me a general. Even though I had had a general once with no problems for one extraction, that was years ago, and I have since had so many life-threatening reactions to drugs that I was terrified by the thought of this operation.

I was thinking about this one evening as I walked home from work, and I suddenly became aware of a presence by my right hand. I turned to look, but there was no one there. The feeling grew stronger, and I felt I could see a figure like Christ walking along by my side. A great feeling of peace and calm filled my being, and all my fear was washed away. I felt a firm conviction that nothing would happen to me and that even if it did, I would be in good hands. This strong presence stayed with me for a few days, then gradually faded. Although I had moments of nervousness about the impending operation, they did not last long, and the memory of that experience kept me cheerful and free of fear through the whole ordeal.

The presence has returned once since then, and even when it is not there I feel as though it will be if I need it, and that is very reassuring.—*D.T.*

Events in the life of M.E. also illustrate this reassuring presence. She was in her 70s, living in retirement with her husband in Arizona. Her husband developed bladder cancer and began following recommended medical treatments which offered good prospects for recovery. Her experience came at what was surely a difficult and tense time.

In April 1989 my husband was to have bladder surgery. We had been told that the tumors were malignant. The afternoon before his surgery, I was resting in our room. All of a sudden—I must have been praying—I looked toward the windows. On the curtain to the right was the form of Jesus. He didn't speak. I was spellbound. Slowly He faded away. He was, of course, reassuring me of His care and the healing of my husband.

I have looked often at the same area of the curtain, but He has not returned there. He has not needed to.

I have wondered why these experiences of Spirit come my way. Could it be that the Trinity of "Divine Love" knows that I am receptive? I know that the intellect will not take us into the way—"but we must become like a little child . . . "

Well, I am just so very blessed and I know not why! Perhaps many others are touched in this way but do not tell others.—*M.E.-Acct. #1*

Here we see Christ manifesting to reassure and comfort her, and possibly to indicate the imminent healing of her husband.

## Physical Danger

Some years earlier, M.E. had also had an encounter with Christ in a life-threatening situation—this time her own. Whereas all the previous stories in this chapter have dealt with illness, this one is a bit different. Here it was the danger of a catastrophic airplane accident. She attributes the pilot's successful avoidance of disaster to Christ's influence. What is certain is that Christ calmed her fears in a profound way.

In 1948, my husband, daughter, and I were living in Paris. He was employed by TWA at their French office. I took a flight to Geneva with another TWA wife. She had been visiting in Paris with her husband, who also worked with our airline.

During the flight we encountered a violent storm. My friend became panic-stricken. She said that she knew we would crash into the mountains and that she would die leaving her four children. I did my best to calm her— speaking of God's care—and suggesting for us to pray. All of this did not calm nor console her.

I closed my eyes and a quietness settled upon me. Then, as clear as a bell, I heard the voice of Jesus. Yes, I *knew* it was His voice saying, "Peace, be still."

At that very moment, the pilot was able to lift the plane up into the realm of safety above the storm. The sun shone so brightly that I seem to remember its warmth coming through the airplane window. I did not mention this to anyone on the plane—I must have been in such a state of joy and fulfillment. This experience is still vivid in my heart and mind after all these years. It makes me recall the story of Jesus calming the storm, as related in the Gospel of Mark.—*M.E.-Acct. #2*

The experiences cited thus far in this chapter clearly indicate that Christ manifests in some situations to heal life-threatening medical conditions. But we are left wondering why such interventions seem so rare. In fact, for some people it might be easier to accept the premature death or the suffering of their loved one if Christ had never been known to intervene at all. When we are faced with compelling evidence that Christ does occasionally manifest in this way, it can be deeply disheartening. We can be shaken by our apparent powerlessness to orchestrate such interventions. We might find ourselves asking, "Why are *our* prayers not good enough? Why do the people in our lives seem to suffer and die without the slightest token of assistance from above?" Instead of serving to deepen our faith, those Christ encounters which grant a few individuals a reprieve from death have the potential, on the contrary, to awaken our anger and cynicism toward God's apparent capriciousness.

But maybe Christ comes principally to heal the spirit, not the body. Maybe in some cases the body responds also, and provides an additional effect to which we may tend to attach greater importance than is warranted. Given the fact that all of us are mortal—that death is only more or less imminent— maybe Christ comes to correct more serious conditions than illnesses and injuries. Perhaps the primary focus for His healing is our need for love and redemption.

This idea gains support in the story of D.H. whose wife was dying from cancer. D.H. remembers:

During the period when my wife was seriously ill, a friend of hers came over to visit one day. My wife was in bed while the three of us talked. Suddenly she started speaking to someone else. It soon became apparent that she was having a party and was greeting her guests— guests who were invisible to the two of us. It was a two-way conversation even though we could hear only my wife's side. She would greet these guests, telling them she was glad they could come, and then listen and answer, sometimes laughing—evidently some of them said things that were funny.

This went on for about 20 minutes, during which time the friend and I tried periodically to convince her that she should relax. She would say that we were right, and she would lie back and be quiet for a few seconds. Then she would continue.

Finally she started saying good night to her guests, saying how happy she was that they made it, always with a two-way conversation. In one conversation, after saying good night, she paused and listened, then made this reply: "Oh, yes, *He* was here. He told me I was going to die tomorrow. Isn't that wonderful?" There was no question about who "He" was from the awed way she said it.

My wife passed away at 2:00 the next morning.—*D.H.*

Most of us experience a wide range of often-contradictory emotions when someone we love is suffering from a protracted and apparently terminal illness. Above all, perhaps, is a feeling of helplessness. Consequently, D.H. must have experienced a great deal of comfort knowing that Christ assisted his wife in her time of greatest need when he himself could do nothing. In that sense, the Christ encounter was for him, too.

Indeed, when Christ manifests during the final hours of a person's life, everyone around the dying person seems to partake of His influence. In the following account, B.G.'s dying father alone sees Christ in the room while his family attends to him. But B.G. and his mother have their own experiences which supplement and verify his father's vision.

My father was dying in the hospital, when I had an odd experience as I stepped out for a walk at noon. As I looked at my shadow, I saw that it was intense black, but surrounded by bright white and ringed by a rainbow about six inches wide. I had no one to share this with but checked several other times throughout the day only to find it was still occurring. When I looked at the shadows of other people, I observed that the phenomenon was associated with mine alone.

It stopped, but on the following Tuesday it occurred again. About that time, my father had a relapse and was in a critical condition again. On Wednesday at 5:00 p.m., he died and was resuscitated. At 9:00 p.m. he died again and was resuscitated. Then, in the early morning hours on Thursday, he had a seizure and was stabilized. At 6:00 a.m. the doctors called to have us come in. When we arrived, my dad was conscious and alert but on a respirator. He was pointing at the ceiling. The nurse who was there said nothing, but we knew Dad was having a spiritual vision. I asked him if he saw someone. Dad nodded yes. "Is it your mother?" I asked. By squinting, he gestured no. "Is it a relative?" Again he indicated no. Then I asked, "Do you feel love, light, and acceptance?" He responded with a glowing yes. "Is it Christ?" *Yes, Yes!* he nodded.

He then pointed at me, then at my mother, extended two fingers in a "V" and brought them together. He then crossed his heart and pointed to the figure. I knew he was asking me to promise in front of God that I would take care of Mom.

Dad began breathing easier, so the doctors removed the respirator tubes. Then, on Saturday morning, my mother and I both awoke with the same dream: Two men dressed in white were assisting Dad to sit up. The only difference was in Mom's dream she was lifting his legs.

When we called the hospital, they said he slipped a little during the night but was resting comfortably. But at 8:00 a.m. or so, he passed over.

That day I again saw the rainbow shadow. On Tuesday was Dad's funeral. I had not been a practicing Catholic for 30 years. When it came time for communion, I heard my father's voice say, "Come, have supper with me." After the funeral, I again saw the rainbow shadow. Mom on several instances has felt Dad's presence; and he has guided her to important papers and keys. He even told her not to worry about her health, as she was fearing cancer. Mom does not worry about dying anymore.

—B.G.

D.H. and B.G. had reassuring and possibly life-changing experiences associated with the Christ encounters of their dying loved ones. But the intensely meaningful experiences were not sufficient to reverse the dying process.

Given how most of us fear death and the loss of those we love, it might be hard to accept that Christ would manifest at all without actually reversing the illness which has befallen us or the ones we love. We would like to have more than consolation—we would like to *survive*. But none of us can escape our destinies as mortal beings. Even Jesus' companions gained no permanent advantage over death. Indeed, legend tells us that all but one of the twelve apostles experienced harsh deaths.

Again and again history suggests that the Divine only rarely seems to alter the material conditions we face. Yet, we can perhaps take heart that His love insulates us against the doubts and fears which prevent us from marshalling our best efforts in the face of adversity. Beyond that, it may also be true that He will assist us—as He did R.H.'s wife and B.G.'s father—in the final transition from this world to the companionship He has promised.

# Chapter Four

# Emotional Healings

A single theme unifies the otherwise richly diverse collection of Christ encounters presented in these chapters. Regardless of whatever else might take place, Christ expresses *profound love* toward the witness in virtually every experience. The way this love impacts a person seems to depend on his or her needs at the time. For instance, we have already seen that if a person is ill, the Christ encounter can promote actual healing or, at least, facilitate the graceful acceptance of one's predicament.

Likewise, as we'll see in the accounts that follow, the same healing process happens for mental and emotional distress. In the span of moments, the Christ encounter can lift a person out of emotional turmoil, leaving that individual free from paralyzing emotions and empowered to undertake new directions in life. The healing seems to take place as the witnesses recognize that they are loved and accepted by a radiant Being who *knows them completely* and who points to a relationship with Himself as a completely sufficient refuge for the "poor in heart."

## The Healing of Depression and Fear

It was during a period of depression that J.D.'s remarkable experience came to her. Despite her emotional state, she said that she had gradually developed a relationship with Christ over a period of months prior to her intense and momentary encounter. Her experience suggests that many Christ encounters occur as a punctuation of an ongoing, developing relationship with Him, rather than as an event unrelated to the witness's prior beliefs and yearnings.

> After years of searching all types of religions and beliefs, I came home to Christ. If He is not the highest entity of God's creation, then He is at least a very high one. He is the Being whom I am most culturally and emotionally able to understand. About eight years ago, He reached out to me and I answered. I'm vague on that first experience. I can't put it into words. It came over time. It was not a bright light experience. It was a relationship that grew, and after a while I looked back and realized that He was real for me.
>
> Then He came to me in an appearance that was sudden, intense, and brief. I was in one of my depressions—one of my crying jags in which I felt totally worthless and unloved, self-hating, and alone. In my black pit there was suddenly a window thrown open, and love and light streamed down on me. I saw the Christ and He said to me, "You are loved." It was there for one clear instant and then it was gone, and I was reeling from it. The depth of my being felt changed.

I have since felt an inner confidence in the love that is there and in the certainty of Christ's reality.—*J.D.*

J.D.'s momentary encounter left her with an enduring sense of Christ's love for her. Obviously, the length of the experience had little to do with the impact it had on her life. We might ask, Why do these encounters have such a lasting therapeutic benefit?

We can answer this question, at least in part, by examining the field of psychotherapy. In particular, several leading spokespeople—like Carl Rogers[17] and M. Scott Peck[18]—have attempted to cut through much of the theory and technique by asserting that "unconditional positive regard" or the underlying assurance that one is accepted or loved is the principal healing force in the therapeutic process. My own experience as a counselor bears this out. It makes sense when we consider that most emotional problems develop around a conviction that one is not loved—for that matter, not even worthy of love.

But while I usually find it possible to express unconditional positive regard for my clients, it is no easy matter to convince them that they are worthy of love. Why? Because in most cases, they know things about themselves which, they feel, invalidate another person's love for them. They are also likely to feel that the other person will cease loving them once the truth is known. They might think, I've fooled them and it's just a matter of time before I'm found out. Understandably, this conviction that one is unworthy of love, combined with the awareness that the other person does not know the whole truth, effectively nullifies the healing force of another person's unconditional regard.

However, in most cases the Christ encounter transcends this dilemma. Consider what happened to J.D. She was somehow able to grasp the immediate fact that Christ's love is based on a complete knowledge of her. His love is profoundly healing because it is a "fully informed" love.

Another woman found that Christ's love did not diminish as He left her, even though she dreaded to see Him go. The witness—a 44-year-old woman—had the following dream twenty years ago:

> I once had a dream of Christ. This dream remains one of the focal points in my life and has carried me through many a dark and frightening hour.
>
> He was in New Jerusalem, attending to a group of people in a balcony-like area. He came to me and did not speak. But with His mind, He told me He loved me, oh so much. I did not speak either but felt if He should move on to other people, I would die. I couldn't bear to have so much love taken from me. I didn't die when He moved on. His love left an indelible mark upon me, and I turned to talk with the others.
>
> Christ's beauty and serenity were indescribable . . .
>
> —*S.L.*

S.L.'s experience brings to mind the resistance many of us have to entering into intensely loving relationships: We fear the eventual loss of the love. Believing that love is exclusive, we feel that if the other person moves on, we will be left with nothing. Given the way many relationships go, this fear is a reasonable one. However, S.L. discovers that Christ's love sustains her even as He attends to others. She learns that His love for her is *deeply personal, but not exclusive.*

As we have seen in so many of the accounts, Christ's manifestation can be quite brief. However short, the encounter typically leaves an indelible memory that influences the recipients for the rest of their lives. For instance, an anxious little girl whose mother had been hospitalized observed Christ briefly smiling down at her from the clouds.

My first experience was at the tender age of 3 or 4

years old. I was at home all by myself. My mother was in the hospital and my dad was at work. I remember going to the window and looking up at the sky, watching the clouds sail by. As one of the clouds came into my view, I saw a Figure appear in back of the cloud, looking down, half-smiling at me. I remember backing away from the window, but I knew who it was even though I know I had never heard Jesus' name or heard anything about Him before then. I don't remember too many events that happened to me at that time, but I never will forget this one experience. I never mentioned it to anyone because I felt no one would ever believe me. But years later I told my children and my best friend about it.

—M.P.

It is interesting how M.P. says that she recognized Jesus even though she did not know His name until some time later. This suggests that the Christ encounter might activate knowledge that goes beyond the experiences we can recall. It also casts uncertainty on the notion that we simply conjure up these experiences out of the raw material of our own memories and beliefs.

While one might doubt the authenticity of this account more readily than some of the others —given the age of the girl and the way that clouds typically activate the imagination—the experience, nonetheless, remains sacred to the 67-year-old recipient today: In the last 64 years, she has told only her children and her best friend. Given her silence, which is typical for Christ encounter recipients, one can understand why this phenomenon has remained largely unacknowledged.

Many of us have done something in our past for which we cannot forgive ourselves. The passage of time may take the edge off of our regret and even render it tolerable, but some of these memories remain largely untouched by time. No matter how many people around us try to alleviate our guilt and remorse—no matter how much we might try constructively to "reframe" our act in a way that makes it understandable if not forgivable—we may still hold ourselves accountable for something that apparently cannot be undone. These situations, in particular, seem to require an intervention beyond the realm of ordinary healing processes. What happens if we cannot forgive ourselves or accept the atonement available from our peers, our ministers, our counselors, or our society? The act becomes for us a sin—that is, something that can be forgiven only through divine intervention or "grace."

The experience of P.G. demonstrates how a Christ encounter can begin to usher a person beyond seemingly inescapable guilt and sorrow. The individual—who is today a 32-year-old artist and mother of three—experienced Christ's forgiveness after having an abortion at age 19.

> About twelve years ago, circumstances seemed to force me into a corner and I made the choice to have an abortion, a decision which devastated me. A couple of days after the abortion, I went to an afternoon movie, trying desperately to run away from my thoughts. I ended up leaving the theater abruptly in the middle of the show and going for a drive into the country, simultaneously crying and singing. I was singing the hymn "In the Garden," when I became aware of a bright light filling the car. It was as if a huge flashlight were shining from above and the beam of bright light was following me down the road. I sensed so strongly the presence of Jesus sitting beside me that I kept looking for Him in bodily form. When the light left, I felt calmed, restored, and forgiven.—P.G. (2)

So many of us labor under the effects of actions that we cannot undo. P.G. experienced what is perhaps the only solution for such unrelenting regret—God's love for us *anyway*.

Just as P.G. experienced healing as she was driving her car, M.L.P. saw Jesus sitting beside her in her car as she "pretended" to be speaking to Him about what troubled her.

> I had been driving down Atlantic Avenue. It was winter and the street was deserted. I had been troubled by something. Often I needed someone to talk to so that I could sort out my thoughts. I would pretend I was talking to Jesus—not prayerfully, but like you would talk to an older brother. No "Thee's" or "Thou's," but straight talk. Suddenly I realized something was happening in the seat beside me. Since I was driving, I couldn't watch intensely but saw a heightened energy pattern. I could almost see Him sitting beside me. His left arm was thrown back over the seat, and He was turned slightly in the seat almost facing me. As quickly as the energy pattern had appeared, it went away. But I knew that He had almost materialized before my eyes. I was awed, of course, but comforted. It seemed that while I had been watching Him, my mind had been put to rest about the problem, and I was left in that peace.
>
> —M.L.P.-Acct. #3

Once again, Christ's appearance serves as a completely sufficient reassurance for M.L.P. Indeed, it would be hard to imagine anything that would be more effective in putting one's worries to rest.

M.L.P.'s attitude prior to Christ's manifestation is particularly instructive. She acts *as if* Christ is present and listening. Her several accounts show us just how this attitude apparently keeps the door open, resulting in an ongoing relationship with Christ, characterized by multiple contacts.

G.T. is another witness whose multiple encounters seem to stem from a willingness to invite Christ into every dimension of her life. Since each of her encounters were brief and related,

I have included them here together, rather than placing them in separate chapters. Overall, the main thrust of her encounters seems to be emotional healing and spiritual empowerment.

Back in 1952, I was married and had a 5-year-old daughter. I led a good but very simple life; however, as a wife and mother I needed counseling and guidance. One morning, while alone in the house, I was praying for help. Suddenly, I had a vision of Jesus dying on the cross for me. I then experienced God in a personal way and accepted Him as my Father, Leader, and Guide.

In 1968, my 13-year-old son fell prey to a freak accident, which traumatized me. He underwent more surgeries in 1969. One mid-morning, I went to a cottage prayer meeting. There, again praying for help, Jesus enfolded me in a big wave of love, in another wave of holiness, and in a third wave of gentleness, while reminding me that His children are harsh with each other instead of being kind and gentle in their associations and relationships. I then became more involved with the downtrodden, the heartbroken, and the underprivileged.

Finally, one Sunday night in 1984, a lady evangelist came to my local church to preach. As she stood on the podium, I sensed and felt Jesus standing by her. He invited me to minister more publicly for Him. He also increased my writing ability.

Since 1969 in particular, Jesus became my Master. Each time He contacts me, He changes me for the better. I reach out to more and more people around me, and they in turn bless me with their love.—G.T.

In G.T.'s experiences, one gets the sense that Christ is teaching and shaping her toward serving Him more and more effectively. Like other witnesses who have experienced multiple Christ encounters, we can see that G.T. has chosen a path of modern discipleship. Christ, in turn, seems even more available to her, serving as the ever-present Taskmaster, Teacher, and Comforter for the duration of her journey. In these cases, in particular, we can see how Christ can assume a variety of appropriate stances optimally suited to assist individuals in their efforts to grow closer to Him and serve Him more effectively.

Some of us suffer from recurring fears and phobias. Sometimes we can trace these fears to traumatic events in the past, but sometimes their sources are unknown. L.H. developed a recurrent nightmare after finding herself living virtually alone while her husband traveled. After experiencing numerous frightful nightmares, Christ appeared at her bedside in the middle of the night. His presence had a twofold effect: The nightmares ceased altogether, and she was never again afraid to be alone. Here is her account:

> Since my childhood I always had a deep belief in God and Christ (Jesus).
>
> I was born in Santa Fe, New Mexico, and came to California at age 16. I married at 18. My husband is from Baghdad, Iraq. When I got to his country, I had no knowledge of speaking Arabic nor Turkish. His family spoke both languages, plus English. My husband's business took him to different parts of the country and I had to stay home with his family. Because of the language barrier and my being in a foreign land, I became lonely and frightened.
>
> I started having bad nightmares, during which I felt something evil grabbing my legs, and then I would wake up. After one of those dreams took place, I experienced my Christ encounter. Toward the early part of the morning hours, before waking, I saw Jesus sitting at the foot of my bed. I sat up and embraced Christ, and He put His arms around me, too. He cradled my head on His shoulder and I wept. Christ said to me,

"Never be afraid because I will always be there with you." I fell asleep again. My nightmares stopped, and I am never afraid to be alone ever since I had my Christ encounter. It was a beautiful experience. Now I am 53 years old. That took place 35 years ago.—*L.H. (1)*

L.H. received the reassurance she needed to deal with her fear in that moment. More significantly, she obtained a promise that Christ will *always* be with her. He didn't say, "— only if you are good." As we have noted in so many other accounts, His promise to L.H. seems unconditional and complete.

We have observed in the *Awakening* encounters that Christ manifests to individuals who have not previously sought a relationship with Him. But it seems likely that L.H.'s deep belief in Christ before her experience might have had something to do with paving the way for her encounter.

Of course, beliefs are a double-edged sword which help to define, if not actually determine, the range of what is desirable and possible. But just as surely, they can determine the extent and limits of our experience, too. In other words, our beliefs can *open the door* to spiritual experiences by affirming a reality beyond ourselves. They can also *impose limitations* on how the spirit can manifest in our lives. Here then is without doubt one of the most difficult and perennial problems facing the spiritual seeker: distinguishing between those beliefs which serve to promote transcendence and those which do not.

## The Healing of Relationships

Interpersonal relationships are the primary source of our emotional turmoil. So it's not surprising that many of the accounts of emotional healing deal with this area.

What goes wrong in relationships? What's the source of so much unhappiness? A fear of never finding anyone who will stand beside us? A doubt that our loved ones will remain loyal to us over time? A fear of rejection and betrayal? These feelings sometimes prevent us from ever taking the necessary risks to find out if an enduring relationship is even possible. There is simply no way to know how we will fare on the other side of committing ourselves to another person.

In the following account, Christ manifests to a teenage girl who was experiencing anxiety about her life and future. Jesus Himself appears and reassures her about her future marriage and family.

When I was a teenager, I had an encounter with Christ. Although I had a loving and supportive family, I still had troubled teen years. I was in the habit of praying every night before I went to sleep. One night, as I was praying, the face of Jesus became so vividly imprinted in my mind that I was compelled to open my eyes and, sure enough, there was Jesus in the corner of my room! But I could only see His face and, although His lips didn't move, He "told" me not to worry—that I would have a husband, one son, and one daughter. He also said that I would have a white house in town (I was living on a farm), and my husband would have a blue-collar type of job, and we would be very happy.

Now I know this sounds completely senseless! But I cannot begin to explain the peace and joy and sense of "relief" that I felt inside of me. Those feelings that night are inexpressible! When I boarded the school bus the next morning, I wanted to shout that I had seen Christ! But I didn't, of course, because I would have been laughed at. I have never told anyone of my encounter. It still sounds crazy to me, but I know it happened. Without a doubt I know that.

A couple of years later I married a boy that I knew was right for me from the time of our very first date. Five years later we adopted a baby girl, and two years after that we adopted a baby boy. My husband was in blue-collar work the first 25 years of our marriage, and his attempt at white-collar management failed miserably for very strange, unusual, and unforeseen circumstances. After much personal stress, he is back in blue-collar work and much happier. The first home we lived in was white, although when we had our children our home was another color.

We have been married 33 years and, although these later years have been a little less than happy, we had an unusually happy life when our children were young.

Christ has never appeared to me again in that way, but I know now how wonderful it will feel to meet Him at the end of my life on this earth.—*A.R. (1)*

As a counselor, I know that the foreknowledge Jesus conveyed to A.R. would greatly assist some of my clients, who have been so wounded by past relationships that they have become fearful and cynical. While it is hard to imagine Christ manifesting in this way to those who are still strong enough to take risks and grow through the process, it is easy to see why He intervenes when hopelessness sets in.

Another woman received similar assurances when she, too, began to feel hopeless about relationships with men.

On Mother's Day, I went to church and was kneeling before a statue of the Blessed Mother. I told her that I was so tired of meeting the wrong men and that I wished to meet the right man for me. While I was praying and crying, Christ appeared beside me. He was dressed all in white. He put His arms around me and said, "Everything is going to be all right now; everything is going to be all right."

I went home knowing that the right man was coming.—*C.W.-Acct. #1*

C.W. had no doubt that Christ's words would come true.

She did everything she could to prepare for the meeting that she was convinced would soon happen. It didn't happen instantly. Actually, she met her future husband at a wedding sometime later. But throughout, C.W.'s faith never waned. Apparently, the encounter was so convincing that she could never fully dismiss His promise. She said, "Once or twice since then I've said to myself, 'Did this really happen?' But He was there with me . . . I believe He was physically in the room with me."

Twelve years later, after going through cancer and other hardships, C.W. had another emotionally healing experience with Christ. While attending a retreat, she experienced difficulty in sleeping. She prayed for help in going to sleep.

> I turned out the light and a bright light came into the room. From it came Christ in white, with the Sacred Heart showing. He was beautiful, but the light was so bright. I watched as long as I could because of its beauty, but finally I could no longer stand the light and got up to turn the room light on to stop it. Up in the corner of the room, I found a picture which I had not seen when I arrived. It was of Christ with the Sacred Heart. There was such a feeling of joy from seeing Him. It lasted for months.—*C.W.-Acct. #2*

It might seem odd that C.W. would intentionally bring an intense healing experience to an end. But as I've discovered from my own experiences, the energies awakened in such encounters are hard to sustain for any length of time. It is as if the physical body and the personality are normally poor "conductors" for the power brought to life in Christ encounters.

Individuals who have been mistreated as children frequently find that it is particularly difficult to resolve the deep anguish of those early experiences. As the adult child attempts to reopen meaningful dialogue with his or her

family members, sometimes it is hard to know whom to hold
accountable. For example, abusive actions are rarely taken
without the tacit permission or gross insensitivity of the other
parent. The one who drank or hit or molested is an obvious
culprit in the child's memory. But the silent, often-unconscious
and sometimes victimized partner becomes, on closer
inspection by the maturing child, a co-conspirator in the
wounding process. This surprising awareness typically
surfaces as the child slowly awakens to a more sophisticated
understanding of how parents tolerate, if not unwittingly
support, their partner's dysfunction.

The witness in the following Christ encounter—a 40-year-
old man—is surprised to discover that he needs to forgive his
mother who, like himself, was victimized by his abusive
alcoholic father.

> My experience was very profound and powerful. I
> must give some history leading up to the day that Jesus
> changed my life! I must tell you some of my experiences
> as a child. From a very young age, I was in the midst of
> extreme turmoil. My father was an alcoholic. He wreaked
> havoc for the whole family, especially my mother. My
> childhood was a nightmare! My father beat my mother
> many times, and I felt like I had to defend her from a very
> early age (3 to 4). I felt like the parent. I had to at one time
> save her life, as I stood between a knife and my mother.
> My father never physically harmed me or my brothers
> or my sister. This is a bit difficult to write to you, even
> now. The fear and turmoil lasted until I was 7 years old,
> when my mother left my father for good. What happened
> to me in those years would be difficult for an adult,
> much less a child. I had so much concern and fear for my
> mother, but I internalized it all. In short, I was traumatized
> many times in total fear for my mother's life. I felt like
> her parent. As I grew older, the traumas from my

childhood took a mental, physical, and psychic toll on me. In my 20s, I sought help for my emotional problems. I even abused alcohol (which as a child I vowed never to do). I went to psychologists and studied astrology, numerology, and took many "new age" courses, trying to free myself from my "fears for my mother." My mother in my late 20s through my 30s and into my 40s would upset me in many ways—even just by her presence. I came down with stomach problems, as well as other physical ailments. I knew intellectually my problems stemmed primarily from my childhood and my relationship with my mother. But I just could not get a handle on how to heal and release these internalized ghosts from the past. In a very real sense my mother lived within me as well as outside of myself.

I was attending an annual conference for the members of the Association for Research and Enlightenment. My experience with Jesus was rather brief, but I felt very strongly that it was He. During the conference, I attended a talk on forgiveness. I was rather tired and almost skipped the talk; but, for some reason, I felt motivated to attend. As the speaker went through her talk, I was sort of "just there"—a bit distracted and not concentrating too well.

Then the lecturer started leading us on a guided meditation about forgiveness. We were supposed to choose a person that we wanted to forgive. I sat for a few moments, trying to pick a person. I thought about an old girlfriend. Then, all of a sudden, it was as if a movie projector went on and my mother appeared. I remember a feeling of surprise and also a peculiar feeling of being a spectator, yet a part of the proceedings. My mother seemed like a little girl, and tears immediately came to my eyes. I wanted to hold her and protect her. All of a sudden, as if behind a huge curtain, a large Figure appeared. There was a very bright light. A Man in a robe whom I could not really make out took my mother's hand and said, "Come now, we must go." My mother like a little girl followed Him into the light. I have never cried so hard in my whole life. My mother, the little girl, was safe now and I knew it, as I sobbed.

Upon returning to the beach house after the talk, I cried for a few more hours. For several days afterward, I felt "spacey" and sort of out of touch. I would not have objectively chosen my mother for forgiveness because to me, at the time, it was clear that she was a victim of the traumas of my childhood as well as I was. The internalized mother has gone with Jesus. And my mother is safe.—*R.H. (1)*

R.H. says that the stomach problems that he had developed due to his constant worry were greatly improved following the Christ encounter. Interestingly, he also found upon his return to California that his experience coincided with his mother taking significant strides on her own behalf: She had decided to move from California to Tucson and had gotten involved in church as well. In both an inner and outer sense, R.H.'s mother had finally left him to pursue her own meaningful course in life, leaving him for the first time free from concern about her welfare.

The effects of childhood abuse can show up later in many ways. Unfortunately, this typically leads to a continuation of troubled relationships. As an adult, the person may too readily accept the familiar abusive treatment that can come from bosses, lovers, or a spouse. It's at this point that a Christ encounter can have a potent, transformative influence. For example, a 44-year-old divorcee experienced a renewal of her self-esteem in the following Christ encounter:

I was the typical product of a severely dysfunctional family unit. There was physical and emotional abuse. I had absolutely no self-esteem at all by the time I had grown up and no education either. I was attracted to an abusive, affection-withholding male and all I ever knew is that I was in pain and denial. I never felt I had any control over my life. My husband spent the marriage trying to convince me I was ugly, stupid, and crazy. I shudder now at the passive role of victim I played.

A friend introduced me to Edgar Cayce's *Story of Jesus*. Many more books followed. I started to feel there was light at the end of the tunnel. My husband's moods, however, became increasingly more depressed. I wanted some love and joy in my life. I was desperately searching for a way out of my hopeless relationship with my husband. I wanted joy and peace.

One night I had a dream. Jesus came to the end of my bed—I did not see His face. I do remember being fascinated by the intricate herringbone pattern to the weave of His garment. There was a lovely glowing light of oatmeal color. He said, "There is joy in Christianity." At that instant my whole being was pervaded with an intense feeling of ecstasy. I remember thinking that this was the way I was supposed to feel. I could never find the words to describe the way I felt.

I awoke completely amazed at the experience, and I knew something extraordinary had happened. I couldn't really believe that Jesus had heard of or come to a non-entity like me. I went to a priest I knew and trusted. He said that I had to believe that I had had an actual encounter with Jesus and that I was very blessed indeed.

I can see now how this encounter became a catalyst in my life. I realized if Jesus had enough esteem of me to visit me personally, then I really did exist on an equal basis with all other souls.

I went back to school for five years and became a registered nurse. My husband and I are divorced. I went into therapy and started to deal with the childhood abuse that almost destroyed me. I have forgiven my parents and am actively working at trying to have a better relationship with them.

I know now that I am choosing all of my experiences on this plane for my spiritual development and I know that the feelings of joy that Jesus gave me are my birthrights and something to work for.—*G.P.*

Letting go of a longstanding relationship can be especially difficult for individuals, like G.P., whose self-esteem has been destroyed in abusive circumstances. Such people often feel obliged to make their relationships work at any cost to them. Yet, once G.P. realized that Christ loved her, her own self-esteem was restored. She was then able to emancipate herself from a union that had become a form of imprisonment and take steps toward her own development.

Another woman who was abused as a child has experienced several Christ encounters. Most of them seem to revolve around the healing of insecurity and anxiety—emotions that have their root in her experience with overly critical parents.

I was having a terrible time with anxiety. I was very nervous because of several unpleasant experiences. One night I dreamed I was in the backyard and I saw Christ walk through the gate. I was overjoyed to see Him and ran over to hug Him. We hugged for a while and then He started to pull away, but I wouldn't let Him go. He said that I had to let Him go, so I did.

A few weeks later, I was thinking how comforting that dream had been, but so very brief—I wished He had stayed a longer time in the dream. That night I dreamed of a Spiritual Being standing in the yard at the side of the house. This Being sparkled and shone as if made out of thousands of brilliant diamonds—I couldn't even make out any features, just an outline of diamonds from head to toe. This Being said, "Don't worry. Christ will be coming to talk to you again."

Since then, I've had several other dream and waking experiences with Him.

On one occasion, I was feeling very depressed and down on myself, feeling that I couldn't do anything right. This emotion was left over from childhood when my hypercritical parents were always pointing out something wrong with me. Suddenly I felt His presence in the room; though I couldn't see anyone, I knew it was He. He said that I shouldn't allow *anyone* to make me feel bad about myself or criticize me. He sounded angry, but I knew the anger wasn't for me, but for the way I had been hurt.

Another time I wasn't thinking of anything in particular, when I heard a voice say, "Child, I am always with you."—*R.R.*

It occurs to me, as a therapist familiar with the lifelong effects of child abuse, that Christ has given R.R. the very thing she never had. He has expressed His love for her and reassured her again and again. He has promised her that He will always be with her. Sometimes we forget just how essential basic assurances of love can be in the healing of longstanding wounds.

K.S. was 22 and in a troubled relationship when she had her Christ encounter. It gave her the reassurance she needed to eventually end the destructive relationship.

I had been involved with a man for many years (most of my adult and teen years), and the relationship was not a healthy one for me or for him. Over the years, we had grown apart. I had been looking for the answer of how to end the relationship or if I should end it. (I've always believed that what God has joined . . . ) One day, my boyfriend and I went bow-hunting deep in the woods.

I was not hunting: I merely wanted to be with him and to enjoy nature. My boyfriend brought me to a hunting blind made of rocks and told me, for my own safety, to stay there until he came back.

I had little with me to entertain myself—just a backpack with some food and apple juice—so I engrossed myself in a study of nature. I really looked at the colors of the leaves, the insects crawling near me, and the glorious blue sky.

At one point, I was meditating on the troubles of my relationship with my boyfriend. I looked up at the sun, partially hidden behind the leaves, and it seemed to pulsate. I saw a face in the sun that resembled Christ's. Being cautious, when I heard a voice speak to me, I asked, "Who are you?" The light vision pulsated and answered, "Some call me Buddha, some call me Christ." I answered, "I don't know Buddha," and He answered, "Then I am Christ." I looked over at my boyfriend who was passing by and I felt love for him, but also felt detached from him. I don't recall most of my conversation with Christ, but I know I spoke of my fear of leaving my boyfriend, of "failing" my boyfriend, of being alone if I left him. The one phrase that I remember distinctly is Christ saying, "I am with you always."

That phrase, that voice, that face has been a great source of comfort to me in the years since then. I have finally freed myself from that unhealthy relationship. As of yet I have not found a new love, but I am confident that he is out there. And that *He* is out there to be with me always as He promised to His apostles and to me, as lowly as I am.

If you would like to know some of my background, I am a Roman Catholic, I currently teach pre-school and Sunday school . . . I attended Catholic school in grades 1-10. I am not a holy person and I don't know why Christ came to me, except to remind me that I need not fear loneliness, for we are never alone—"I am with you always."—K.S.

Christ doesn't say to K.S., "You don't need men; you only need Me." He lets her know that whatever happens, His love will not abandon her. Obviously, He offers a *different kind* of relationship in which K.S. can find the security often lacking in ordinary human relationships.

The Being's answer to K.S.'s question, "Who are you?" underscores our difficulty in conclusively identifying the Being who appears in some of these encounters. The Being does not say that He is Christ *or* Buddha: He implies that He is both at the same time. From the ego's point of view, it is easy to make the mistake of concluding that this Being has no intrinsic nature—that He is a spiritual chameleon who only mimics the beliefs of the witness. To the ego, it looks too much as if the Being has *no* identity if it can't be an *exclusive* one. This "need" for exclusivity overlooks the possibility that Christ is a Being whose inclusiveness allows for many names.

It just goes to show us how we, as individual egos, build our identities through *excluding* aspects of ourselves rather than *embracing our wholeness.* To the ego, being everything is a form of death; for there seems to be no way to preserve our distinction in a state of oneness. But that's *our* problem, not Christ's. Perhaps we would do well to acknowledge our limited thinking rather than insist that He be more like us.

In an account similar in effect to K.S.'s, a 32-year-old woman was feeling the loneliness that comes from knowing that an emotional relationship is over. Again, Christ manifested to remind C.A.M. of His enduring love for her.

I was at a very low point, at the end of an intense personal relationship. My male friend was throwing a "welcome to spring" party one Friday night, and I knew it would be too wild for my frame of mind. I, therefore, made arrangements to stay at a hotel for the night.

I settled in for the evening, complete with book, food, and TV. As I compared the differences in my emotions now as to when I first met the person, the most glaring awareness was "I'm alone again. I'm alone again, and I've accomplished nothing. Here I am, right back where I started. Has all that I've gone through here been for nothing?" As I sadly thought this, the room changed subtly. A feeling of utter peace descended, and to the left where the balcony and sliding glass doors were located, the area brightened. I felt a Presence fill that area and a feeling of being absolutely loved welled up in me, swept over me. I knew it was Jesus. I mentally heard a voice say, "You are not alone. You have Me." We communicated, then the Presence withdrew, back out the doors where He had first entered. I was renewed. I should add that the significance of the balcony is that beyond it lies the ocean, which has always held a lot of meaning for me.

Rough circumstances followed, but I'm still holding on to the faith this experience instilled within me. From that night on, I feel that the course of my life was redirected, reshaped. I discovered an inner strength that was lacking before I heard the simple declaration, "You are not alone."—*C.A.M.*

Another woman experienced Christ's intervention in her troubled marital relationship quite differently. Instead of experiencing Christ coming to reassure her of His love for her, she dreamed that Christ extended Himself to her alcoholic husband. When her husband in the dream sent Christ away, the woman became convinced that the relationship should be ended.

Several years ago I was married to a service man who was very jealous of me, even though I gave him no reason to be. In one of his drunken episodes, he told me he had better never find a strange man in his house and that included my minister or Jesus Christ Himself.

He was transferred to Germany and the CO thought Paul would do better if we—myself and three children by a former marriage—were with him. So we went.

One Saturday, Paul went to the base and I went back to sleep and had this vision. A knock came at the door and I opened it to find a Man who said He was Jesus Christ. I asked Him in to sit awhile. Then Paul came in and asked Jesus to leave his house. Jesus left, but returned to tell Paul we only wanted to help him, not hurt him.

Within two months I and the children were back in the States, and I divorced Paul.

About three years later I married a wonderful man. We went to a lake one night to fish. I was in a chair, looking up at the beautiful sky, and a voice asked me to forgive Paul. I told Him I have forgiven him, for I knew he was sick.—*M.E.B.*

As M.E.B.'s account indicates, the experience of Christ's enduring love can help a person accept the end of a troubling or destructive relationship. In time it may also facilitate the actual forgiveness of the other person, even though this may not come for years.

Besides providing the emotional support individuals usually need before terminating a destructive relationship, Christ's intervention can also apparently *improve* a relationship by removing some of the obstacles which stand in the way of deeper trust and intimacy. In the following account, the witness experiences relief in two areas, one of them directly related to her marriage:

I joined a charismatic prayer group at a time when I was open to my spiritual life. I was in a state of excitement and grace while at the same time aware of a spirit of fear.

I felt this fear at night when I would walk down the hall from my room toward my newborn daughter's room to nurse her. It was a fear of the dark and an "evil" presence.

I was also in the process of deep contemplative and persistent prayer, requesting God for a healing that would positively affect my sexual relationship with my husband.

One morning between 4 and 6, I "awoke" to a feeling that penetrated my very being with a warmth and a joy that was overwhelming. I opened my eyes and saw Jesus "hovering" or floating before and above me as I lay in my bed. His arms were stretched out and opened—as if welcoming me or blessing me.

I recall vividly the love in His face . . . I felt I was looking at His face with my soul. His face and upper body were visible and translucent, but His body was covered in a flowing robe.

Love was radiating from His face into my body, and I felt it physically as warmth and glow and throbbing vibrations. The best way to explain it in human terms would be a spiritual-sexual experience.

Since then, my fear of the dark has lessened, and I have come to realize that I am capable of experiencing orgasm. I do not know if there was any connection between my experience of Jesus and my prayers in this regard.—*M.M. (2)*

M.M.'s encounter with Jesus apparently healed her on at least two levels. Yet not a word was spoken. The evidence of His love was, once again, completely sufficient to activate the healing process.

One cannot deny that sexual relations are of crucial importance in maintaining most healthy marriages. Even so, some might balk at the idea of Christ manifesting to heal sexual dysfunction. Before embarking on a debate over this matter, it is best to remember that we can never be sure of the Christ figure's intention. After all, just because the Christ encounter has a particular effect on the recipient does not mean that it intervened only to address that condition. On the basis of dozens of Christ encounters included in these chapters, all we can really say with confidence is that the Christ figure expresses an almost overpowering love for each recipient. Perhaps we experience healing wherever it is needed, whenever we contact such profound and total love. M.M.'s sexual feelings during the encounter were, from this standpoint, merely the indication of where the healing was needed, not necessarily an indication of Christ intent.

Sometimes relationships end without any closure when two persons part ways without one of them letting the other know the full truth of his or her feelings and the reasons for leaving. For years thereafter, it may be hard for those who were left behind to let go and move on, as they wonder whether they did the right thing or whether they could have done something different. This rehashing can effectively prevent one from moving forward into new relationships.

In the following encounter, Christ manifests ostensibly to assure the recipient that she had done well in a relationship in which the other person had apparently left before she could arrive at any closure:

I had my second Christ encounter following a relationship with a man who hurt me very deeply.

During our relationship, I put my own pain in the back of my mind and took care of him, for he was in very bad shape psychologically. After he left, I had doubts. I knew I had done the right thing, but I wondered if I had done enough.

About this time, I had a dream in which I was walking

along the Sea of Galilee. The Master approached me and He took something—I don't know what it was—and pinned it on my lapel, right above my heart. What I remember distinctly was the ring on His hand. It was gold with a square, and in the square were sixteen round amethysts. It seemed there was assurance I had done well in that relationship. I just remember looking at that ring as He was pinning on the object.

Years later the man came back to me and said he was sorry for what he had done. That closed the chapter.

—R.J. (2)

R.J. experienced Christ's gift as a symbol of completion, which finally freed her to release the old relationship. This dream brings to mind the importance of rituals and ceremonies as ways to signify concretely the end of a learning process and the inauguration of a new phase. Recognizing the power of such enactments, many modern psychotherapists assist their clients in setting up such rituals in order to obtain closure in a relationship with a person who has disappeared or died. Depending on the individual's need, anything from writing letters to addressing the deceased at the gravesite can serve as effective ways to obtain closure when the other person is unavailable.

## The Dark Night—
## Turmoil Brought On by Spiritual Awakening

Sometimes when we adopt new, higher ideals or affirm a closer, more committed relationship with God, our lives begin to take a turn for the worse. All of our unfinished business from the past comes back to haunt us—our regrettable choices, our hurtful actions, and our unresolved pain from old relationships. We find ourselves looking in the mirror at a person who has failed time and time again to respond to a higher calling. The awareness that we have fallen so short can be enough to make us conclude that we are hopeless. *We become depressed because we have awakened to our "fallen state."*

J.M.S. experienced Christ coming to her following her slide into a depression of this kind. Interestingly, He does not deny the "grayness" of her life but instead calls her to follow Him through it.

My membership with the Association for Research and Enlightenment was only a few months old. However, my interest was at its peak. I began to meditate and pray, attempting to draw the light of Christ from within myself. In meditation I found warmth and peace of mind, harmony and relaxation. Out of meditation, however, I found myself introspecting and analyzing different areas of my present life with some amount of criticism and negativity. The "snowballing" effect of those few weeks of intense introspection consumed me with depression, doubt, fear, and anxiety. Worst of all, I found myself feeling unworthy of the Father's love.

In the midst of this suffering and burdensome consciousness, Jesus came to me in a concise and vivid dream. I stood in a narrow, white hallway with a doorway at the end. Jesus stood in the doorway dressed plainly in a simple, long white robe, without sash or embellishment. Behind Him was a grayness or gray cloud. The very second my eyes met His, He turned. The symbolic movement meant everything to me! The impression I immediately received was "Follow Me and have faith." The grayness Jesus turned on to shocked me, for I expected a path paved with gold . . . but my path with Jesus has its crosses, and I believe His manifestation was so that I could find strength in Him and carry on.

My perception on everything the next day and since then has taken on a new light in the grayness. My love and spiritual awareness of our Lord only deepens with time.

The Christ encounter I experienced was not engulfed
in light and glory, but the message was clear to me.
                                                —*J.M.S.*

As we have observed in so many of the Christ encounters,
Christ's appearance signaled a new beginning for J.M.S.,
even though the path ahead looked nebulous and somber in
its grayness. But with every significant new beginning, there
is a death of old ways of thinking and being—a fact easy to
overlook as we contemplate the "good news" of His coming.
Yet, the recipient of the following dream encounter was
painfully aware that change involves a "dying" or a letting-
go process as well.

I dreamt that I was on a pier with my brother. We
signaled with torches to someone out in the water. Then,
as we signaled again, my face became the other torch. I
was not in pain, just burning. Later, I was alone, having
been reduced to just a living skeleton by the fire. But I
was not able to die. A friend—someone I'd known
through church activities—tormented me. He did not
recognize me. First, I tried to identify myself. But then I
realized I didn't want him to find out who I was and tell
my family; for I was concerned about their reaction. So
I left and went wandering around the land, through the
streets of towns, looking for a way to die. My body and
face were covered by a hooded robe, so no one could see
me.

Later, I learned that Jesus was nearby, teaching crowds
of people. I wanted help from Him, but I didn't want to
come face to face with Him. I was afraid His followers
would confuse me with something evil. Then, I saw
Jesus teaching on a hillside some distance away. So I
went to a hillside across the valley, from which He was
only barely visible in the distance. I reached out with my
mind to Him from across the valley. He heard me and

turned toward me to look my way. I knew that He completely understood my plight. At that moment, I died. My bones fell to the ground, and I was finally freed from the bondage of that living death.—*K.L.*

This dream might seem puzzling and even disturbing in its dramatic imagery. Yet its meaning comes clear with some help from the witness. K.L. says that while he had been active in church all of his growing-up years, he had been "sitting on the fence for a long time and was in no hurry to get off." As an engineer, he came to value only those things which could be verified through physical observation. Consequently, he "was still filled with questions and doubts which I didn't expect to be able to answer with any degree of certainty or proof." The dream effectively underscored his state of spiritual stagnation and pointed to the necessity of "dying" or letting go of the old self. Yet this is difficult to accomplish on our own. When trying to orchestrate our own transformation— in the spirit of "wanting to change"—we can only get so far before we find ourselves caught between two lives, unable to let the old self die completely and allow a new self to emerge. Deeply committed to Christ today, K.L. says that he believes the dream came to serve as an encouragement to acknowledge the place of Christ in his life.

Some individuals experience depression because they possess a heightened sensitivity and concern for the collective problems of humanity. Their depression and despair seem to originate, at least in part, from sympathetically taking on the plight of the disadvantaged and grieving for the senseless acts of violence and carelessness in the world. Of course, these feelings are particularly hard to resolve, since the amount of control that one individual can exert over the collective situation is virtually nil. One such person, whose other Christ encounters are included in Chapter Six (M.B.— Accts. #2-#4), obtains relief by having the situation meaningfully "reframed" by Jesus Himself.

In this dream I felt I was actually in Christ's presence.

We had watched "Jesus of Nazareth" on TV the night before. I was feeling very depressed because of the then-pending threat of a nuclear catastrophe at Three Mile Island in Pennsylvania. I was praying that night for the return of Christ so that humanity could again learn from Him.

I fell asleep and dreamt I was with Jesus and a few other men. We were in a building that had woodworking tools in it—to make designs on legs of furniture. Jesus was teaching us, and I began to cry for humankind. Jesus came up to me and said I should not worry—that the vibrations of humanity were being raised. He then cut some threads that surrounded me. I couldn't see them, but He said they were there. He then turned to one of the men and asked him if he saw silver when he cut. The man very excitedly said, "Yes!" Jesus smiled. He was very beautiful.—*M.B.-Acct. #1*

M.B. says the dream was a real turning point for her. "It really made me acknowledge Jesus as the Master. It also helped me to realize that it was in times of turmoil that humanity turned to Jesus." The cutting of the threads can also be seen as the necessary severance of her excessive emotional connection with disturbing events around her.

C.R. was in the midst of inner turmoil. She was emotionally "bleeding and broken." In this state of vulnerability, she experienced Christ's presence on several occasions, beginning with a dramatic vision of the crucified Christ. It is as if His own suffering conveys a full recognition of her pain and casts her personal struggles against the backdrop of His own meaningful ordeal. Once again, her depression seems to stem from an acute awareness of her own "fallen" state, not from some external, temporary condition. It is a form of depression which is hard to overcome because it is based on an accurate perception of her own spiritual condition.

I started having experiences with Christ during the summer of my 18th year. Prior to that time, I was an atheist. During that season, however, a Catholic friend was helping me find Jesus.

The experiences started one morning. As I awoke, I saw a glowing white hand in front of me with a hole in the palm. The hand moved toward me and, instead of stopping at my face, it went through it and touched me behind my eyes. I immediately experienced a tingling sensation throughout my head and neck and saw our Messiah in front of me as clearly as one might see a person in the flesh. I saw Him bleeding and broken, for I was emotionally the same at that time. When the vision faded, I looked at the carpet where He had stood and saw footprints in the carpet that seemed to glow white. I told my sister and mother about the vision, and they also saw the footprints.

I was going through a great deal of inner turmoil during my late teens. As time went on, I noticed that Jesus often appeared to me, though not as vividly as our first encounter. While I feel Him often throughout the day now, I usually don't see Him clearly unless I am suffering deeply.

At first all this frightened me: I thought I was losing my mind. However, in 1982 when I was thinking these thoughts, an impression came to me, "For you, this is normal," and that comforted me.

From 1975 to 1989 I was severely depressed. I feel that these experiences have helped me enormously in overcoming my depression.

I have seen with my own eyes the infinite compassion of our beautiful Savior, how understanding, wise, and faithful He is to us even when we don't return that love. I have had to struggle with several besetting sins for years, and His willingness to understand and forgive inspires me to emulate Him. I learn from His patient example, and what I appreciate most about Him is that He is so humble—He never makes one feel as if one were beneath Him even though He is Lord of Lords. This was especially important to me during my depression, because I felt so worthless then.—*C.R. (2)*

C.R.'s ongoing emotional ordeal calls to mind the lives of well-known Christian mystics—like John of the Cross and Teresa of Avila—who, as a rule, underwent periods of extreme hardship, despair and/or depression. Sophisticated Christian thinkers have come to view this "dark night of the soul" as a necessary stage in the spiritual journey rather than an embarrassing footnote in the lives of otherwise devout individuals. It is a period in which the seeker comes face to face with his or her fears and recalcitrant nature, and struggles to bring this nature into alignment with God.

In her exhaustive research on Christian mysticism, Evelyn Underhill—author of the classic *Mysticism*[19]—observes that the dark night of the soul typically begins *not before but after* the mystic's initial illumination. It is as if the bright promise of that first awakening brings a person's less lofty characteristics into stark relief. The need to understand and integrate the less-than-exalted side of oneself may account for why the Christ encounter does not always eliminate one's struggle in an instant.

As we have seen in several of these Christ encounters, Christ assists the healing process by making the ongoing ordeal more meaningfully related to the eventual goal of union with Him. Given the immensity of the task of overcoming lifelong emotional patterns, it may even be that it is the quality of the struggle—not its complete resolution— that prepares a person for partnership with Him.

## Chapter Five

# The Beginning of Initiation— Confrontational Christ Encounters

**M**ost of us share an uneasy fascination for stories of great tests of courage and faith. Jesus, in particular, faced numerous tests just before and during His public ministry. In the desert, He was tempted by the worldly power He could have enjoyed. He turned it down. Later, He had to confront the ignorance and betrayal of His followers and friends. When He needed their companionship the most, they slept. He prayed alone. Finally He was given an opportunity to save Himself by denying He was the Son of God. He said nothing to dispel this claim and was killed for it. Clearly Jesus remains for us the highest example of an *initiate*. He faced and surpassed the most difficult tests imaginable, remaining devoted in an uncompromising way to His Father's work.

Few among us would welcome the kinds of tests Jesus Himself faced. But individuals who have sought a closer relationship with God sometimes welcome the opportunity to demonstrate their love of God and their readiness for a closer partnership. Indeed, the idea of spiritual initiation has a rich history in the religious traditions of both East and West. In the East, stories abound of gurus orchestrating puzzling ordeals designed to deepen their disciples' humility and spiritual understanding. For instance, the Buddhist guru Marpa made his eventual successor, the great guru Milarepa, build and then tear down a house over and over again. Milarepa found Marpa's ambivalence frustrating and utterly puzzling; but he complied, nonetheless. He was eventually rewarded when Marpa conveyed his teachings upon his obedient disciple.[20]

There are many examples of spiritual initiation in the Old Testament. God commanded Abraham to sacrifice Isaac to see if Abraham would put anything before his allegiance to God. Abraham showed himself willing to obey, and Isaac was spared. In a less obvious situation, one can discern an initiation test unfolding when Joseph is betrayed by his jealous brothers and sold into slavery. He demonstrated the depth of his character not only by the good works he performed in captivity, but also by his eventual forgiveness of his brothers. In one of the most obvious examples of initiation, Job's lengthy ordeal provides us with a view of a Deity subjecting His servant to seemingly unwarranted tribulations before finally rewarding him for his faith. Through these and other examples, we can see that the God of the Old Testament comes across as a Deity who severely tests those who are, presumably, already doing a passable job at giving themselves to His service.

In contrast to the Old Testament God, Jesus Christ extended His acceptance and love without making His followers undergo formal tests or initiations. He chose ordinary, uneducated men as His disciples without applying any obvious test of their readiness. Once accepting them, He then proceeded to treat them as fully adequate disseminators of His teachings.

But He did not overlook their weaknesses either. On several occasions, He subjected them to the kind of challenges that resemble initiation tests. In the most brilliant ways, He awakened both His followers *and* critics to unacknowledged blocks that prevented them from accepting the full mantle of discipleship. Yet one doesn't get the sense that He judged them unworthy—only that He could see clearly in them the self-imposed barriers to a closer relationship with the Father. For example, Jesus didn't turn the rich young man away, but gave him a choice between following Him and retaining his wealth. The young man *chose* to turn away, realizing that his attachments were more important than the path to follow Jesus.

Similarly, Jesus didn't command the vicious crowd to spare the prostitute. He simply encouraged them to explore their own consciences for evidence of their sinfulness. Nor did He tell the three apostles who witnessed His transfiguration on the mount who He was: He asked them— as a measure of their faith and understanding—who they believed He was. In another instance when Jesus told Peter that he would deny Him three times before the cock crowed, one can sense more than just a foretelling of events: Jesus was confronting Peter with his weakness and challenging him to overcome it. Though Peter failed that test, it is easy to view this failure as an initiation experience that served later to bring the best out of him.

Throughout the Gospel record, we find that Jesus labored

to awaken people to what they had placed above their relationship with God. It should come as no surprise, therefore, that many of the Christ encounters that we have collected echo this theme. They reveal a Christ figure bringing unfinished business to light so that the witness can resolve it and come into a closer relationship with Him.

In some of these reports—which I've termed *Confrontational* Christ encounters—the process of initiation begins, but remains incomplete. In these accounts, the witnesses encounter a situation that brings to light an unresolved problem, but they do nothing about it during the experience. They're left feeling like King Belshazzar, who saw the mysterious writing on the wall. They realize that they have "been weighed in the balance and found wanting." (Dan. 5:27)

In these accounts, the Christ figure may not be present at all. If He is, He may appear angry or stern as He lovingly confronts the witnesses with unresolved problems. The emotional effects of this confrontation can be quite unsettling. Even so, the confrontation points promisingly to a closer relationship if the witnesses can remove the self-imposed barriers between themselves and Christ.

In other reports—which I've termed *Initiation* Christ encounters—the witnesses are able to take the process further. Instead of reacting in a habitual way to the problem being presented, they're able to respond appropriately to it *during the encounter* and resolve the problem before the experience ends. Once this corrective response is made, the experience typically culminates in a full encounter with Christ.

*Confrontational* and *Initiation* Christ encounters are the same except for how they conclude. As they unfold, they exhibit the same twofold purpose: (1) to awaken the person to an unresolved problem and (2) to elicit from the witness a response that resolves the problem. For whatever reason, some people are up for the challenge, while others are not. It might be useful in the future to examine the differences between those individuals who succeed and those who fail in meeting the tests presented. We might find, for example, that those who succeed engage in regular prayer or meditation as a way to foster spiritual surrender. Or we might discover that they are involved in intense interpersonal relationships where they can receive regular honest feedback concerning their own restricting habit patterns. Knowing what makes the difference could help us take some steps to increase the likelihood that we will respond appropriately if, and when, such challenges arise.

## Who Confronts Us?

Initiation implies that someone is involved in setting up the test. *Who*, we might ask, is examining and testing us? Does Christ Himself actively confront and challenge us? Or could it be that as we begin to open ourselves to His all-loving presence, something within us creates the test? This latter case would entail our becoming aware of all we've done that blocks accepting ourselves as worthy of His love.

The accounts indicate that both cases might be true. If Christ lives within us—perhaps as our own true natures— then the initiation test proceeds out of ourselves. But since Christ also remains an Other Person as long as we have not fully "arrived," then the test can seem to come from Him as well.

Throughout this chapter, we'll examine a series of *Confrontational* Christ encounters—challenges which might have developed more fully if the witness had managed to respond to the test differently. In the next chapter, we will examine several *Initiation* Christ encounters in which the witnesses were able to pass through the tests and find communion with Him.

## *Confrontational* Christ Encounters

Many of us would like to meet Christ face to face. But if the following account is any indication of what we might experience, some of us would be turned away—not by Him, but by our own lack of readiness for such a relationship:

> I write concerning a "confrontation" with my Higher Self and Christ that began with a dream.
>
> I awoke shortly after 1:00 a.m., sitting bolt upright, crying "No! God, No!" as I seemed to be forcibly thrust from His Presence. A powerful, unforgettable stream of love came from Him as I went out. Immediately I began repeating a phrase I recalled from the dream— "monoclearite vision"—and was interrupted by a loud, emphatic voice saying, "Not Clearite—clear-eyed." I then recalled the entire scene: I was facing my Higher Self, whom I recognized from an earlier encounter, who was in front of and central to and to the left of Christ.
>
> Christ, who was not visible to me but appeared as a formless dark shadow, asked, "Is this one ready?"
>
> The Higher Self replied, "No, he is not."
>
> Christ then asked, "Does he have 'monoclear-eyed vision'?"
>
> Then I answered, "I know what it is, but have not been practicing." Then, I felt banished from their presence.
>
> Again, 28 years later, I awoke hearing a clear, gentle, authoritative voice ask, "Are you ready?"
>
> Having singleness of purpose has been an elusive pursuit as my attention span is like a child's. My intentions are solid, but sometimes I do not persevere diligently. However, I still feel the force of His love beamed at me even as I left His Presence, which brings me back to a more focused practice of prayer, meditation, patience, and service.

Except for that beam of love, this was a devastating experience that left me in shock for some time afterward. And to some degree, I still am.—*W.A.*

W.A.'s experience must have been shattering—to have entered the presence of Christ only to discover that he failed to measure up to that relationship. Similar experiences of the Grail knights are told in the medieval Arthurian legends.[21] Like W.A., a few of the most exemplary Grail knights managed to gain entrance into the castle of the King Fisherman. It was the resting place of the Holy Grail—the cup Jesus used during the Last Supper.

But even after getting that far, all but one of these knights failed to pass the final test of their allegiance. They were dismissed from the castle because—while they witnessed the Grail in all of its radiant splendor—they failed to ask a simple question. Entranced by the cup's beauty, they stopped short of going one necessary step further. They neglected to ask: "Whom does one serve with the Grail?" They failed to offer themselves to what the Grail served—or to serve the King Fisherman Himself! Like W.A., they lacked "monoclear-eyed vision"; that is, the singular ideal needed to take them through all the tests. Only Percival asked the crucial question, and he alone became the King Fisherman's successor.

In W.A.'s experience, Christ's "judgment" in this *Confrontational* encounter occurs in a context of unquestioned love for him. It is a juxtaposition rarely encountered in ordinary life. Usually if someone judges us, we feel unloved at the same time. The simultaneous awareness that one is both loved and found wanting is a hallmark of the *Confrontational* and *Initiation* Christ encounters.

W.A. felt banished, but he was not banished by anyone other than himself. His "banishment" came in realizing that he did not have what was required of him. Similarly, the following *Confrontational* encounter —which is one of my own—was apparently arrested by my hasty flight from the frightening dream scenario. I, too, realized that I did not have what it took to deal with a frightening test. In this Christ encounter, Jesus exhibits an attitude which is both loving and stern as He assumes a highly confrontive stance toward me. I had this experience in my late 20s, and its implications left me sobered.

It is interesting that Jesus explains the reasons for subjecting me to the unpleasant experience before the ordeal begins.

> I dream that I am returning from a long journey. I know that I have been wayward and indulgent during the time away. I carry a large, ornate, silver cross studded with gems. I support it against my side, much like a Catholic priest might carry a large cross during a procession.
>
> I walk down a dusty street of a primitive village and turn the corner only to see Jesus standing with a group of men. They all face me with stern expressions. Jesus says with love and firmness, "I have come to show you what you have built. The only reason I do so is because your father wants Me to and because I do this so well." As I stand puzzled by this, He hurls a flame-tipped lance toward me. Passing through my sleeve, it impales my arm against a wall behind me. Then He throws another one, which anchors my other arm.
>
> Immediately, I find myself in another place—in a battle or in a gladiator's arena. A large, mean man in a cloth headdress (like the ancient Egyptians or Sumerians once wore) stands over me. He proceeds to tell me how he is going to kill me. Realizing that I must be in a dream, I force myself awake.—*G.S.S.-Acct. #1*

Clearly, in the dream there is no resolution to the dilemma I faced. Instead of working through the problem in some way—by perhaps responding to the gladiator in a creative, less fearful manner—I did the natural thing and escaped by waking up. I knew, however, that I would have to deal with this issue before I could have a closer relationship with Christ. As such, the dream presented me with an unanswered challenge—an initiation test that awaited an appropriate response from me. As one might expect, I found less dramatic but essentially similar tests subsequently arising in my *waking* life, giving me repeated opportunities to deal with this issue.

What was the issue? I came to realize that the encounter with the warrior represented, on the one hand, the need to deal with my own repressed urges as represented by the gladiator. I also realized that he symbolized authority figures and aggressive individuals who would awaken in me a sense of powerlessness. With this realization, I came to view my waking life, too, as an arena for confronting this important challenge.

Like my own *Confrontational* experience, most Christ encounters occur in the privacy of one person's dream or solitary vision. Because such accounts elude scrutiny, scientifically minded researchers often object to the study of subjective visionary experiences. They argue, quite reasonably, that there is no way to prove that the event has any objective "life" of its own apart from the person's own fantasy. Phenomena such as near-death encounters, dreams, out-of-body experiences, Christ manifestations, and other meaningful but private experiences all fall into this gray area of scientific research, simply because they lack the one item that would grant them the status of "real"—being observable by more than one person.

However, in the following *Confrontational* account, two persons witness the manifestation of Christ—one from the private confines of a dream and the other in ordinary waking consciousness.

I am a nonprofessional counselor. I do not seek those who may be assisted by my efforts, but let "coincidences" tell me whom I should assist. Invariably, as in this case, I receive as much or more than I am able to give.

Several years ago, I was working with a family who had reached a very low level of hope, mental health, and material circumstances. As this family undertook their comeback, they became active in one of two conservative, rural Christian churches that had been providing material assistance. On occasion, when the father of the family was working on a Sunday, I would take the balance of the family to this particular church, and so I was aware of the congregation, the service, and other particulars. Having scratched the bottom of the pail and started back up, this family was amazingly open to things of the Spirit. A resurgence of their faith allowed them to be happy with a very conservative church and a quite fundamental religion, while at the same time being totally open to the ideas of Edgar Cayce, Yogananda, and others. These folks were, therefore, allowing things to happen and accepting of them if they did happen. In this atmosphere and with frequent sessions in their home, we shared many unusual, special events. So much for the background.

One Sunday morning, I had stayed in bed. The family had a ride to church, and I had led a home service the night before. So I was content to lie back on Sunday morning. I dreamed, however, with unusual clarity and focus that I had indeed gone to that same church. The minister was at the pulpit up front in this middle-sized building, while the roughly 37 people attending were, as usual, crowding the rear of the church, filling up the back three pews. A large open and unused area existed between the minister and his small but loyal congregation. The minister was speaking in an unusual manner—for he was criticizing the members, begging them to show more spirit in the service, in the church, and in their lives. Unusual as this was for the controlled clergy in this church, there was more. For, seated alone, about four pews from the altar rail in the middle of the pew and on the right side of the church was a robed Figure. I could not see His face, which was partially hidden by the robes He was wearing. Somehow the robe also covered His head and shielded His face, save for a direct face-on encounter. But I knew He was crying. And I felt or knew that it was Jesus. As I tried to study this out for myself, my dream was interrupted by the telephone. It was the mother of the family in question. She said she had just returned from church, and she had to tell me about something unusual that had happened there.

She told me how the congregation had sat in the back three pews with all the space between them and the minister. She said the minister preached a very unusual sermon, begging the congregation to allow more spirit in their church, their worship, and their lives. She also said that she saw a Man in church who was robed and sitting on the right side, up front, about four pews from the rail. She couldn't see His face, but she knew He was crying, and she felt she knew it was Jesus. She wanted to know my interpretation of what she had experienced, but I could only tell her about my most unusual dream. Even today, I would welcome more information on this "visit."—S.C.

This story is remarkable because of its independent verification, which is missing from most Christ encounters. But it's also unusual because Christ's apparent reason for manifesting is expressed indirectly through the agency of the minister. There is no *direct* confrontation between the Christ figure and either witnessing party, only a sense of Christ grieving the lack of spiritual commitment from those present.

But, in essence, this is really a confrontational test. Both individuals were forced to see how they might be falling short of the mark.

The following dream encounter bears a striking similarity to S.C.'s. Again, instead of confronting the witness directly, Christ appeals to an audience of which the dreamer is not a member.

> . . . I would like to share with you two experiences I had in my pre-teen years.
>
> In a dream an unknown boy, who is about my age, and I are shown a map with directions for going to Burma. While looking at the map, we have a sense of flying. The next thing we know we are in Burma, with tall grass and elephants, and dirt roads and paths. We turn and walk into a hut. It was a huge room made of adobe-type walls. The boy is no longer with me. I don't see him anywhere. The room is full of people—one can hardly move it is so filled. There's a big party going on with drugs, booze, and everybody getting crazy.
>
> I turn to the north wall and see some steps starting to appear. I watch until they are in full view. Then Elijah and Daniel come down the stairs with Christ following behind them. Elijah and Daniel stop at the bottom of the steps and Christ stops a few steps behind them.
>
> Christ pleads with the people in the room to follow Him, that He is the way and the light, and they should throw away their worldliness.
>
> No one cares; some even laugh and jeer. He keeps pleading, but it is no use.
>
> Elijah and Daniel turn and start back up the steps, ahead of Christ. He takes a few steps, but then He falls down, weeping very deeply. Elijah and Daniel then turn to aid and comfort Him. He was weeping because He knew the people were lost.

They do not listen, and my heart feels very heavy as I begin weeping, too. Then we (the boy and I) are home again. We turn and look at each other in complete shock.

The whole dream did not have any spoken words to it, even when Christ was talking. I felt and knew what He was saying. I wasn't there as a partaker; even though I was in the crowd, I felt separate from the crowd.

A second dream occurred a little while later. I really don't remember how much later. It could have been a few months or maybe about a year, but no more than that.

This second dream starts with my climbing a very steep mountain. I hear someone calling me; I don't see anyone, but He keeps calling me. I finally look up and there is a light, a very warm light. I can't see His face, but I know it's Christ. He then reaches a hand to me. I can see the marks from the nails. I reach up to take it, but as I do, the rocks go out from under my feet and I fall. It's a long fall; but I experience no fear.

I fall into a river, a very deep and wild river. I can't swim, but I am helped. I don't know how, I just feel the help. I get to shore safely. I start to climb the same mountain again. I get about two-thirds of the way up, then I look up, and at the top of the mountain is a golden cross with brilliant lights showing all around it.

The dreams more or less started my spiritual journey.—*V.O.*

Given the pre-teen age of the recipient at the time and the additional challenges that have faced adolescents since the late '60s, one can see how these Christ encounters came at a crucial moment in V.O.'s life—perhaps to counteract a possible tendency to give way to the excesses of the day. While she feels that she is not a "partaker" during the Christ encounter— just as S.C. merely watches the robed Christ figure in his dream—one has to assume that Christ's intervention was meant as much for S.C. and V.O. as for the audiences in their dreams (who are, one can argue, aspects of the dreamers).

Even if the witnesses were not falling short in their commitment *at the time of their experiences,* the encounters are nonetheless tailored to offset any tendencies in that direction. This observation leads us to an important conclusion about Christ encounters: They exert a *preventative,* if not also corrective, impact on the witnesses. One can say that the *Confrontational* Christ encounter comes not only to point out past errors, but also to arouse a vigilant response in the witnesses that will counteract future threats to their spiritual unfoldment.

V.O.'s second dream, though superficially dissimilar to her first one, again points to the struggle to maintain her singular commitment to Christ. The repeated falling away captures the cyclic struggle of many of us. We find that the spiritual journey consists of periodic breakthroughs interspersed with regressions to earlier unresolved issues. The wild river, like the teeming hedonism of her first dream, perhaps underscores the constant tension between the ego's waywardness and the soul's sincere desire.

Surely the problems posed by *Confrontational* accounts are significant. If they are important enough to warrant Christ's involvement, then our responses to them probably exert a significant impact on our lives. In some instances our responses could be a life or death matter. For example, one of my own *Confrontational* Christ encounters hinted strongly that my very life depended on a willingness to do what I was "called to do." Without actually telling me that I might die, Christ seems to point out the inevitable—that avoiding my own path might unwittingly undermine my reason for living.

I mentioned the following account in the Introduction, but it bears repeating in more detail here because it demonstrates just how serious the *Confrontational* Christ encounter can be:

I am with Mark, and we are both aware that we are dreaming. We begin flying crisscross patterns through a large new auditorium, as if we are preparing it and consecrating it. We actually interpenetrate each other as we simultaneously pass through the center of the room.

At one point I see him standing in a doorway at the back of the auditorium, talking to Someone behind the door. I know it is Jesus! Anxiously, I walk through the door and look toward Him. At first I am only able to see a bright white light. But then the light abruptly changes into the clear form of the Master.

He looks just as I would expect Jesus to appear, except His hair and beard seem quite dark, and His features sharper. He seems stern, but I feel His love for me. As I stand there, saying nothing, awed by His presence, He asks, "Are you ready to leave the earth yet?" Startled by the implications of His question, I say, "No." Then He says, "Then go out and do what you know to do."

—*G.S.S.-Acct.* #2

Jesus did not have to tell me that I was failing to measure up. His question left no doubt of that. Yet His attitude was so loving that I could feel that there was actually no judgment coming from Him. Instead there was only a loving intent to point out my apparently precarious hold on life due to my failure, up to that point, to heed my own deeper calling to serve Him.

I did not say, "Of course, I will do it." It took me a long while to come around to that! Even today, I struggle with this. Yet, in some encounters of this type, the witnesses responded to Christ's initial confrontation with a "corrective response" within hours or days of the experience. By so doing, they essentially converted a *Confrontational* Christ encounter into one of full initiation. For instance, one 12-year-old girl had a remarkable pair of experiences that demonstrated the impact of a corrective response. In the first she was confronted with God's wrath. Then, chastened by the overwhelming experience, she remained in a prayerful state for several days afterward and took symbolic measures to cleanse herself. This response then seemed to pave the way for a harmonious culmination in a subsequent Christ encounter. Writing in mid-life about these events, she reports:

> When I was around 12 years old, I decided to tease my sister Dorothy. I piled dirt clods on the cover of our outdoor toilet and waited inside for her to come to use it. As she emerged from our house, I threw some of the clods at her. Trying to elude them, she finally broke and ran back to the house. I jumped off the toilet seat and reared back to throw another clod at Dorothy. She ran to the left to escape me. Just as I was about to let go and hit her, I heard a voice. (While it took only two seconds for this to happen, it takes a while to explain the voice and my experience which ensued.)
>
> This Voice sounded like thunder or like hearing a great waterfall, as if the sound were passing through water—like waves. All the Voice actually said was, "Drop that." These words were Spirit as they entered me; they were pure Wrath. They washed through me from the top of my head out the soles of my feet. I immediately began to try to open my hand and found that I couldn't do it. I struggled several times to open my fingers and couldn't. I felt destruction all around me and realized I could be destroyed on the spot. I recognized this Voice as God.
>
> Because I trusted God . . . I found myself trusting Him regardless of whether I lived or died. As I submitted to Him, I felt His words turn to pure mercy. This washed over me again from top to bottom. The mercy seemed to enter my heart like a trickle at first. Then, like a dam

breaking, His mercy flooded my heart and being. His words turned to pure Love. This washed over me the same as before. This Mercy and Love seemed to run together with the mercy and love I knew, and we were one in Spirit. I felt as if all the love, mercy, and justice I ever knew was a drop and He was the ocean. His word was the source of all love, mercy, and justice. I felt as if I came through it only because I submitted and only because of the mercy of God. When I submitted and quit trying in my own power to open my hand, all of a sudden, I felt like a puppet. My hand opened by His power and the clod fell out. I turned around to see where the Voice came from. It had come from the North. I looked and saw nothing. I felt this great sense of redemption, as if I'd been bought at a great price. I then heard Mom calling me.

Later . . . I dreamed that my feet were dirty and I was outside. I heard my phone ringing and I went to answer it. When I did, I found myself at a dinner. There were white tables and plates. I sat down and ate two bites (which I believe to mean the two words that God spoke earlier to me). Then I asked to help serve and was told, "Yes, but why are you dressed that way? You have to go and change." Then I returned and served the table. I awoke and thought that that was an odd dream.

For guidance on the dream, I opened my Bible and it fell to the guest who came to dinner. I then felt a strong urge to wash my feet. They appeared clean, but nonetheless I washed them in a pan of water.

I felt very prayerful for the next four days. I went to bed early one night to pray. Just as my head touched the pillow, I saw clouds in front of my eyes, and an opening came in the clouds. I saw myself standing before an altar with a wooden cross behind it. I closed my eyes, thinking this would go away, but then I saw a "Man of Light" who looked like sunlight. He was in the form of a man. I called Him Shiolah, as if I knew Him. I also heard a still, quiet voice say, "The Christ."

I then saw a lamb work its way from my heart and run to Him. He stood there with His arms outstretched; and this lamb (who I knew was me) leapt into His arms. He petted and stroked the lamb. The vision went away and then came back. Then the Man of Light stood by a sheepfold. He set the lamb into a fold at His right side by His feet. They all were in a green pasture and all ate in His light. He was the only light— all else was darkness. The lamb who was me ate in the green pasture. The Man of Light stooped to pet the lamb, and when He did, I almost lost sight of His face. He straightened and looked at me, there on the bed, and wrath came into His face. Then it left Him, and He held out His arms to me again . . . —D.B.

Taken together, these two experiences run the whole gamut from thoughtless act to confrontation to corrective response to forgiveness and reconciliation. D.B.'s story serves as a good bridge between this chapter's focus on confrontation and the next chapter's focus on initiation. From Christ experiences like hers, we can see a single process operating in both *Confrontational* and *Initiation* encounters. It is a process in which the witness first becomes starkly aware of what stands in the way of a closer relationship with Him. Even though the would-be initiate rarely has the presence of mind to respond immediately and appropriately to the test as it is presented, he or she is often left knowing what needs to be done to resolve the impasse.

So we come to this conclusion: The *Confrontational* Christ encounter points to the future. It suggests a wonderful culmination to the development process which for the moment is still blocked. For now, the relationship with Christ is limited—not by Him but by the witness's inadequate response to his or her own unfinished business. We can regard those who finally makc an adequate response as initiates. They are individuals who meet and overcome a longstanding impasse in their lives. It is their experiences that are considered in the next chapter.

# Chapter Six

# The Culmination
# of Initiation

Initiation is often associated with a journey into an unknown realm—sometimes into the underworld itself. From Ulysses' seaward journey home through Percival's quest for the Holy Grail, the storyline is similar: One must confront and *respond appropriately* to difficult challenges in order to prove oneself ready for fuller companionship with God.

As the experiences in the previous chapter indicate, it's not easy to respond appropriately to the tests of a *Confrontational* Christ encounter. Typically, the would-be initiate is overwhelmed by anxiety or other emotions that get in the way. This confusion often prevents the seeker from responding in a new way to unresolved problems. But sometimes an individual manages to come through with an appropriate response to the tests presented. What often begins as a frightening confrontation can culminate in an ecstatic experience of Christ's presence.

Some initiation tests can, on the surface, seem unreasonable, unrealistic, and downright disturbing. For instance, a 61-year-old nurse was cleaning her home one day when she heard a distinct voice issuing from what felt like the "back of her head." The voice asked if she would leave her family and follow Him. Clearly, M.M. was put to a most severe test of her faith.

It was a beautiful sunny January morning and I had just finished the household chores in the bedroom. I started to go into the hallway when a definite voice came to me. The voice said, "Are you really ready to follow Me?" Without question I answered, "I thought I had been following You all of my life." Then the voice said, "If I ask you to leave your husband, children, and everything you know, would you do so?" I was literally stunned at the question He had asked. Without a shadow of a doubt I was sure it was Jesus who asked the question. So for the next six weeks I prepared myself, my [adult-aged] children, and my husband. It wasn't that I loved any of them less—but if I were called, I had to go. I described as best I could what had happened. It was really very final.

When I was finally ready, I was in the same place in the house where I had heard the voice the first time. I said, "Yes, I am ready to follow." Instantly, I knew I would not have to leave my family. It was the Abraham-Isaac story all over again.

Then the voice said, "Get back in the church. You cannot change it from without." I had been putting off joining a church in my new locale, but immediately did so. Eventually I became an elder in the church and in 1981 started a study group there.

The second thing the voice asked me to do was to make amends with my sister. She and I had never gotten along. I began writing her letters telling her why. I tore up many of the letters, but that was the process of first getting my anger out. Eventually she came to the study group with her friends.

The voice also said, "Find Paula and get to know her." Paula was the daughter of my brother who had been killed in the Air Force. She was born two weeks after he was killed. I wrote her a very long letter and made a trip to see her. We stayed up many nights going through old family pictures.

Years later, when I was president of the American Holistic Health Association, I had a very difficult time with several of the board members. Then I had a vision. I can still see it. It was of Jesus coming down toward me from a small hill with His disciples in the background. He held out His arms, hands together, and said, "Put it in My hands." I did, and things became better. I feel He is with me at all times now.—M.M. (3)

M.M. had served Christ for many years and didn't think it unreasonable that He would ask her to follow Him regardless of the sacrifices required. Yet her commitment to Christ was put to a severe test: "Will you leave everything and everyone and follow Me?" Isn't this what many of us fear God would ask of us if we could hear His promptings? Most all of us can relate to the rich man who was challenged to give everything away and follow Jesus: It would be a hard choice, considering the importance of the people and possessions in our lives. A childhood friend of mine expressed this fear some years ago by saying, "I would give my life to God, but I'm afraid He'll send me to Africa." She was eventually able to take a leap of faith and pursue ordination as a minister. She has never been sent to Africa, but she obviously accepted that risk at some point along the way.

Everything Christ says to M.M. represents a test to see if she can overcome her ingrained assumptions about her church and family members. Each time, she responds by letting go of old ways of thinking and then acting to resolve unfinished business. M.M. is a model for us—an example of a modern initiate willing to do whatever it takes to follow Him.

Even though Christ didn't command her to leave her family, M.M. had to face possible ridicule and harassment from those around her as she went through her preparations to leave. Facing the interpersonal and social consequences of her allegiance to Him would have been a continuing test for the rest of her life. Similarly, a teenage girl suffered months of social fallout from her Christ encounter.

The following is my experience of seeing Christ at the age of 14:

I had entered my freshman year of high school having been elected to the high school cheerleading squad. During the very first game of the season, three other cheerleaders and I were called over to the sidelines and given cups filled with Coke. Appreciatively, I took a sip and found it to be laced with liquor. Instead of disposing of the cup at that point, I finished the Coke but did not have anything more to drink afterwards.

On Monday morning, all of the cheerleaders were called to the principal's office and seated in a semicircle with me at the far right end. Starting to the left, he individually asked if we had consumed any liquor during the Friday night game. Slowly, individually, each one denied she had done so. Then it came to my turn. As I looked into the principal's face, I saw the face of Christ. My words somehow do not fully describe it all. The vision was beautiful and very much real. A feeling of tremendous love, acceptance, and warmth overcame me. His eyes were so loving and intense. The emotions that swelled up within me were overwhelming. I, too, had decided to deny the incident, but after seeing Christ, I broke down and cried. I admitted to the incident during the game. I cried, not because of guilt or a feeling of shame, but because of the tremendous love and acceptance that I felt. There was no fear of what disciplinary action would be taken against me.

For weeks, strength, love, and acceptance sustained me. I was suspended from school for three days and suspended from the cheerleading squad for the first half of the season. Since we lived in a very small community, I also experienced the effects of small-town gossip. Yet through it all, the love, acceptance, and strength was something I had never known before, nor will ever forget.—C.R. *(3)*

Interestingly, C.R.'s whole experience hinged on a quick decision that had to be made. Her momentary flirtation with deceit gave way to a full willingness to admit to what she had done. Christ's love, not His judgment, made C.R. aware of the error of her imminent lie. Her atonement, then, was a completely free, willing act. Through her honesty, she became an initiate. She reaped the inner strength and security she needed to offset the social stigma that followed her confession.

So often the *Initiation* encounter confronts the witness with an opportunity to join Him at the possible expense of leaving behind comfortable aspects of one's current life. M.M. had to face leaving her family, and C.R. had to give up her reputation in a small community. Similarly M.B. was willing to accept the commitment that came from her Christ encounter. In this case the resistance doesn't come from friends and family in her waking life. Instead, she meets it in the characters in the experience itself. A young mother at the time, she was called in a dream to join Christ in battle.

Before I went to bed, I was reading in the Gospel of Matthew, where Jesus showed His disappointment with Israel.

I dreamt that I and about five men were waiting for Christ's Second Coming. He rose up out of the water. He was wearing a beautifully colored striped robe. He spoke with us for a few minutes, and we were to follow by His side to fight somewhere. Somehow I got left behind with two of the men. I didn't realize that Jesus and the others were leaving. I got frantic and I was trying to figure out how to get to Him. The two other men had purposely stayed behind because they were afraid to go into battle. I yelled at them for their lack of faith saying, "Don't you realize the Lord will protect you? And even if you die you will go to the Father. Why do you doubt and fear?" They realized I was right. We got a ride and found Jesus.—*M.B.-Acct. #2*

The dream shows M.B.'s willingness to follow Christ wherever He leads her. Yet she faces a struggle with less-willing aspects of herself. The two men—most likely parts of her more recalcitrant self—provide a convenient opportunity for her to dialogue with this less-than-eager side of her personality. As a result, she is able to bring *all* of the aspects of herself into alignment with His purposes for her.

The same woman discovered in another dream encounter that she had little choice but to turn to Christ to deal with an evil man. Like so many of the *Confrontational* and *Initiation* experiences, she came face to face with a disturbing reality. When she found it too strong for her to master, she called upon Him to assist her.

I had this experience two months after my youngest child was born. It had a very strong effect on me. I actually felt His presence. It was a real turning point; I finally turned myself over to Him.

I dreamt I was in a hotel-type place with many doors. A man entered my room acting very strange, talking about Satan and how he was Satan. I said I didn't believe in that sort of negativity. He had some small heads that had horrible satanic faces on them. He dropped them on the floor, and I casually kicked them out the door. He became more and more violent until he actually killed a man with a spear in the hallway.

I began chasing him and eventually fighting with him to try to keep him from hurting people. As I chased him down the hallway, he was killing people as he passed.

We wound up outside the hotel in a carport area with a group of people standing there watching him. He was becoming more and more powerful and I couldn't fight with him any longer; he was too strong. His voice changed to a horrible deep voice and he was rolling around on the ground. His face was all contorted.

I finally realized I could not fight him any longer and the words, "If ye would but call on Me, believing, I will be there," came to mind. I knew if I called Jesus, He would come. My whole body was tensed up as I screamed as loud as I could, "Jesus, Jesus!" The people said He wouldn't come and I said, "Yes, He will because I believe He will." I just knew with all of my being that He would come. I kept screaming His name and all of a sudden everything became quiet. A silvery, white shaft of light appeared down from the sky. I could make out a filmy Figure in the shaft of light, but I could see clearly His arms outstretched. He said something directed toward the man, and the man rose up smiling and normal, and then said something about the equality or the value of women. I can't recall exactly what He said. The baby woke me up crying. I may have awakened her with my shouting in my sleep.—*M.B.-Acct. #3*

M.B. experiences Christ's power to redeem a most unsavory

character. It all seems to hinge on her extraordinary faith that He would, indeed, come to her. Even though the dream ends harmoniously, it's important to ask, "Who or what was the disturbed, evil man?" After all, dreams like this happen to many people.

At least two answers come to mind. First, he might literally represent Satan or the independent embodiment of evil in the world. As a mystically oriented Christian, M.B. may have underestimated the power of evil in her life.

Second, the disturbed figure could represent a view of men as chauvinistic and domineering, since the man—once exorcised—apparently acknowledges women as equals. Regardless of such an interpretation, the message to M.B. was clear: She could not single-handedly defeat the evil in her life. She had to invite Christ into the situation. Her willingness to surrender to a higher power is perhaps the best response to any initiation test.

As we have seen, an *Initiation* encounter can determine if a person is willing to put a relationship with Christ above the opinions of others. A university theology professor tells of a Christ encounter which took place during his college years. It followed a series of preliminary experiences which tested him and prepared him for the eventual face-to-face encounter.

> This is the account of a unique happening during my college years:
>
> I had been secretly communing with God under the form of Christ—that is, using an abandoned "Bleeding Heart" portrait of Him (and candlelight, before which I kneeled) in the basement of the dormitory for how many months, weeks, days, I do not remember. But eventually the dormitory director discovered me in my secret place and, to my surprise, asked me whether he could join me in prayer. For a while we used to commune there together. In those days, I was deeply into a form of

Christ-mysticism. Christ became my daily object of adoration, and the wind became the Spirit of God against my face.

One day it so happened that I came to commune with God seven times. Although I do not recall the context of every event of communion, here are three of them:

It all began when a rather verbose but brilliant young idealist suggested that several of us gather at 6:00 a.m. in front of the library to pray for the state of the world. It was barely light when I got there. No one else came. Sad I was, but I prayed anyhow; and just when I was about to leave, a strange wind came upon the leaves on the ground and gathered them around my feet. Perhaps this is not an unusual occurrence, but at the time it seemed that God was saying "Hello!" I returned to the dorm.

Later that day my girlfriend and I went to the chapel to pray together, for we had resolved that there would be no sexual relations before marriage; and we shared the challenge to resist together through prayer and mutual confession.

Far into the evening, I was alone in my room when three students, all drinkers, dropped by and asked to come in. I obliged them, but soon they were making fun of what they perceived to be my consistent religiosity. They took my Bible and began tossing it around among themselves. I instinctively reached for it but to no avail, as they taunted me about my religious faith and my overheard verbal witness to the wonder of Christ.

Finally, when left alone, I prayed before I went to sleep.

Sometime around 3:00 to 4:00 a.m., I was lying on my right side, and I simply and calmly opened my eyes. Standing there was a barefooted Being in a long garment, the upper part of which I could not really see. I intuitively sensed that this was neither an ordinary figure nor an ordinary occurrence. For the Figure—which I sensed was male—took His hand, which seemed unusually larger than any normal adult hand, and placed it on my shoulder. Then He gently squeezed my shoulder in His hand three times. But the distinct feeling was that the strength in those hands was so great that even an uncalculated squeeze would have crushed my shoulder completely. Yet the unforgettable awareness I had was that I was being told not to despair or discontinue searching for Truth. It was a literally comforting spiritual experience somehow related to the seven encounters with God during the previous day, although I did not think of this until later reflection upon the event.

I have meditated on why I was not led (or allowed?) to see the face of the Figure, and my thoughts have usually settled upon the idea that I was not spiritually ready to do so.

The wonder is that from beginning to end I knew that it was Christ whom I had encountered.

The next day, when I met my special friend, I discovered something that proved to be an amazing follow-up to the previous night's happening. I could greet her and talk with her about anything but the experience I had had. For when the moment came for me to share the event with her, I could absolutely not speak a word about it, even to the point of crying and facially giving the impression that I was choking on a bone in the throat. Every attempt to even begin to tell her of the encounter ended in vain, as we sat upon the steps of one of the out-of-the-way stairways of the library.

She reached out to help me, as it seemed I was being strangled at my every renewed effort to testify to her about it. Yet there was an almost immediate release from that constriction once I relented from making such an effort.

Eventually (and I am sorry that I do not know exactly when) I was able to testify about the event. I later realized that it was not merely a gesture of comfort but a form of anointing of my soul for a special work in behalf of the advancement of His kingdom on earth. I was eventually to enter the pastoral ministry and departed the little church I served in Arlington, Virginia, only after a memorably successful ministry. I had been called ultimately to enter academia (what I tend to call the "teaching ministry"). To this day, notwithstanding that I have seen many little miracles along the Christian way, that experience stands unique among all my experiences with God as the most significant, long-lasting, and confirming one that I have come to treasure.—W.B.

It's significant that in each of the events that he could recall, W.B. faced a challenge and then responded with prayer and acceptance. One gets the sense that he could have arrested the process at any point by simply giving in to ordinary, understandable reactions to the trials and temptations he faced.

Did W.B. *earn* the visitation from Christ through his exemplary behavior? Or did he simply remove the barriers which normally prevent a person from experiencing an ever-present greater Reality? These questions go to the heart of how we understand the redemptive role of Christ. Is He active as initiator and judge? Or does He simply stand at the door beckoning, waiting for us to remove what stands in the way?

The following lengthy and richly detailed account illustrates the first of these two options: It reveals Christ taking a very active role in the initiation process. He introduces Himself without invitation and aggressively challenges the witness to relinquish her resistances to Him. Her account suggests that

Christ works vigorously with at least some individuals. For her the series of encounters led to a level of commitment and effectiveness far beyond her previous experience.

The witness—a Jewish psychotherapist—first had a series of *Awakening* Christ encounters in which Jesus introduced Himself to her in a comforting and loving manner. Then, once the relationship was established, she underwent an initiation test: Essentially, Christ calls on her to go deeper into her spiritual practices, but she resists. Things get worse as she continues to hold back, until she eventually accepts and undertakes the work she is called to do. The relationship with Jesus is strengthened through her cooperative response to Him. Then later, she experiences herself as a channel of healing for a friend.

S.K.'s multiple Christ encounters are presented here as a single account since her series revolves around a dramatic initiation process.

> I am 49 and work as a psychotherapist. I also do some writing and have the apparent ability to do healing through the laying on of hands.
>
> I am Jewish, yet am strongly drawn toward the mystical and metaphysical. It took me about 25 years of seeking before I found a way to integrate Judaism with my other beliefs. Now, after the experiences I will describe to you, I find myself once more struggling to integrate something new.
>
> Three years ago, I had an experience in which Jesus appeared to me several times during the course of a week. I would be doing something, such as going for a walk, and there He would be, looking at me in a loving way. There was an attitude, more than verbal communication between us. He seemed to be expressing in a kind, loving, gentle way, "What took you so long?" On a conscious level I wondered what that meant, yet at some deeper level I seemed to understand.

The experience left me feeling protected and safe, along with an interest in Jesus. Being Jewish, I really hadn't learned very much about Him.

In looking back at the encounter, I am surprised at how casual I was about it. It seemed rather odd but somehow natural. I didn't tell anyone about it at the time. Three years later, my experience with Him was markedly different.

I had been going through a very busy, pressured week. At night I would get into bed quite exhausted. One morning during this time I was awakened by something or someone. It felt as if I had been shaken awake, but not in a very gentle way. It was 4:00 a.m.

I felt compelled to get up and meditate, but I didn't want to. I was too tired, but something wouldn't leave me alone. Almost against my will I got out of bed and went into the other room where I meditate. I really couldn't figure out why in the world I was doing this.

Soon after I was in a meditative state, I was aware that to my right side was the presence of Jesus. This time His attitude was much more serious, and I started receiving messages about ways I was needing to change. I was to meditate regularly (I'm rather lazy about meditating), do certain exercises first, and make some dietary changes.

The 4:00 a.m. awakenings continued for about a week or two. I was in a very uncomfortable state of mind and body. I was quite frightened. This was not the gentle, benign type of experience I had with Him previously. This was very serious. I felt out of control, as if I didn't have a choice.

My sense of reality was being threatened. How could Jesus appear to me? Why me of all people? Being Jewish made the whole experience even more disturbing. Where was this leading? I wondered if I were going crazy.

The lack of sleep coupled with the emotional stress

took its toll. I started having problems with my body: swollen glands, sore throat, a lump under my arm along with various aches and pains. I was one confused, frightened, unhappy woman.

Finally, I "made a deal" with Jesus that if He would stop awakening me at 4:00 a.m., I would make a commitment to meditate daily. With that, the awakenings stopped, but it took me approximately another month to regain my emotional and physical equilibrium, and I'm still processing it.

About two weeks into the experience, I suddenly found myself starting to feel sad for no reason that I could consciously identify. The sadness welled up in me, and I found myself sobbing uncontrollably. These sobs were so intense they racked my whole body. The feeling that went along with the tears was one of severe grief to have been separated from Him for all of this time. The crying continued for a long time, and, although the feeling of grief was clear, I (the "I" whom I identify with) couldn't understand what was happening. It is as if a different "me" or part of me is having these experiences and I'm somehow not able to fully connect with that part.

The feeling I was left with was that in some way I knew Jesus or was close to Him or believed in Him at some distant time, and for some reason I was separated from Him or perhaps turned away from Him . . .

All of this has led to my working on myself psychologically and spiritually. I have been meditating much more regularly. I'm working at making the dietary changes, reading more spiritual material, and generally working harder at being more loving.

During the time of the "contact," I found myself becoming quite psychic, and a number of my clients commented on how well the sessions were going. It was surprising to me, since I was in such a state of exhaustion. I believe that at that time I was infused with what I'll call the "Jesus energy."

I had one last contact with Jesus about the second or third week after the nightly visits. I was doing an on-hands healing with Peter, a man with whom I am very close. He had been having severe problems with his eyes for about two months, had been to a couple of doctors, and had tried different medications, but his eyes were getting worse. By this time the whites of his eyes were almost all red.

During the healing, I felt Jesus come up behind me and put His hands over my hands. I "heard" that Peter should stop all the medication he was currently using. He was to put castor oil in his eyes nightly and take certain vitamins. In five days his eyes would be healed.

I wasn't sure whether the advice came from Jesus or whether I had made it up. I've done many successful healings in the past but had never had this kind of experience with advice. I told Peter what I had heard and shared my doubts. Castor oil in the eyes seemed scary.

Peter was feeling fairly desperate and was willing to try it. After two days, his eyes seemed worse. I was very concerned that I had harmed him in some way, yet he decided to continue. By the fifth day his eyes were healed. He commented that they were better than they had been before.

I am appreciative of the opportunity to share this material . . . In many ways I have felt very alone with it. As one can tell, I am still filled with doubts and fears as well as wonder about it. I'm not sure where it is leading. As I've slowly healed from the shock of it, I find I'm filled with two conflicting feelings. One is relief that the awakenings have stopped and that my life is back to normal, but the second is that I miss Him.—*S.K.*

This account has a disturbing implication. It suggests that Christ—at least in some cases—does not wait to be invited into our lives but can enter unbidden to impose a relationship and an agenda. Some of us would gladly submit to His will, and we envy those who have felt His tangible presence. Others, however, might feel violated by this intrusion.

But notice that Jesus never inflicts pain on S.K. She begins to experience discomfort only as she resists a growing pressure to enter into a more disciplined practice of meditation. Jesus doesn't make her anxious or frightened: She becomes that way as she avoids the process of growth that has been activated. Then, she feels relieved and empowered when she finally follows His promptings.

In all initiation encounters, a choice is implied. It's a choice between making our relationship with Him the top priority or letting something else assume greater importance. In the following dream experience of a 45-year-old civil servant, the choice is evident. He refused to allow career opportunities to lure him away from allowing Christ's will to prevail in all matters. Then, after passing this test, he is able to go on to pursue the very career opportunity that previously competed with his commitment to Christ.

> I was in a cabin at a retreat center in Buckeyestown, Maryland, attending a spiritual conference.
>
> I recorded this dream at 11:45 p.m., shortly after going to bed. This is the only instance I can remember of receiving a meaningful response to a deliberately sought dream experience.
>
> The speaker at the program, George Ritchie [author of *Return from Tomorrow*, which concerns his famous near-death encounter with Christ] had asked us throughout the weekend to keep a question in mind, which in my own words was, "What is the first step I should take to

learn of Christ's work for me in this life?"

I dreamed that I was praying, "Only as it is according to Your will, be it done unto me. Be it done unto me only according to Your will."

In the dream, it seems that my boss at that time is preparing a proposal for me to get a promotion. She's getting information from me and also from the person who became my boss when I was promoted seven months after this dream. Neither is saying anything directly to me but they're both hinting a lot in my presence. I am praying as above, "Only according to Your will, be it done unto me. Be it done unto me only according to Your will."

I go off to pray somewhere, more to be with Him than to plead for His help.

It seems as if I'm lying on a bed somewhere in a room of an old farmhouse. The room seems to be painted white and so is the outside of that wing of the house. I tell Him, "There's no one else I can talk to but You." At that point I break into tears. I question and berate myself for the tears. Why should I cry? Then I see His face smiling at me. He understands. We both start laughing, and I say to Him, "There's no one else I can talk to but You." He says it along with me in some kind of non-verbal way, laughing with me and delighting along with me in the joy of my new discovery. Then the dream ended.

The promotion did come as a result of the actions of the two people in the first part of the dream. My recollection is that my new boss approached me out of the blue seven months later and asked me to work for him at a higher grade level. Even though I usually deliberate over such decisions, I immediately accepted the job without any hesitation.—*W.M.*

Something unusual is at work here, since the identical career opportunity actually arose some months later. The dream can be seen as an initiation test to see if W.M. would defer to higher authority. Having surrendered his will in the dream state freed him to act decisively when the opportunity arose. Once he had shown himself willing to submit to a higher will, he was then free to pursue the advancement without endangering his spiritual life.

## Appearances Can Be Misleading

People who believe in a Second Coming of Christ are often divided over how this event will take place. Some believe that Christ will manifest physically, leaving no doubt whatsoever that He has, indeed, returned. Others believe that the Second Coming will be a spiritual experience, perceived only by those who can open their hearts and minds to Him. Even if this question could be answered, there is still another one to consider: Will He manifest as the Jesus who walked the earth 2,000 years ago or assume a more contemporary form that may go unnoticed by those looking for the Biblical figure? If Christ comes in a modern form, then our ability to *recognize* Him will be a crucial test of our understanding of His teachings. Having to look beyond the outward appearances of His return may constitute one of the most fundamental initiation tests of all for those who profess to serve Him. Basically, it's a test which determines if the *form* of Christ's manifestation is more important than the *essence* clothed by that form.

This dilemma confronted a 26-year-old man. He encounters a Christ whose unconventional appearance is presented as a challenge in itself.

I had a dream in which Christ appeared to me. Before the dream began, there was a thought-transference experience. It wasn't an actual speaking voice, but it "spoke" and said, "This dream is a symbolic message not to be taken literally." The dream then began.

I received a message that Jesus was on a speaking tour

of the United States and that He invited me to accompany
Him for two weeks. I accepted by returning a letter to
Him. I was subsequently sent to where He would be.

I felt as if I were in the wrong place, but something
reassured me I was in the right place. I knew that I just
needed to look for Him. I started wandering around this
circus—that's why I didn't think I was in the right
place!—it was a circus. I soon found a sideshow tent
with a sign proclaiming, "Speaking Hourly! Jesus of
Galilee! Come See the Savior in Person! Admission
Free." Again this voice came in the dream and reminded
me this was all symbolic and not to be taken literally. I
went on inside the tent. The tent was empty, but there
was a stage up front and there was a stagehand there. I
explained to him I was supposed to meet with Jesus and
that He had invited me. As soon as I said that, the
stagehand's face brightened up and he said, "Oh yes!
He's expecting you. But the show is about to start. You'll
have to wait until afterwards."

People were coming in, and then Jesus came around
a curtain and saw me just as I saw Him. Although I knew
it was He, I was surprised at His appearance. Instead of
the traditional Christ figure, He was wearing a gray pin-
striped suit. He was bald—His face didn't look like the
traditional Jesus face. Actually He resembled my uncle
Ed. I knew unquestioningly, however, that it was Jesus.

He greeted me and apologized for having to rush
right into the performance—I guess you'd call it that. He
gave me a glass of something to drink—lemonade or
something. After a few moments an announcer walked
out on stage and said, "The show is about to begin. And
now here He is—the one and only—Jesus the Christ." It
kind of reminded me of Johnny Carson's introduction.
He began to speak. His words to me were like gold, but
I don't remember the specifics of what He said. I only

remember I was just hanging on to every word.

After a few moments one fellow in the back of the tent said, "Oh, what is this?! I came to see a show not hear a lot of talk." Jesus very tactfully replied that he was free to leave at any time. Jesus continued. Several others got up and left, grumbling and muttering. There was obvious skepticism, but some were really impressed. Others showed no doubt. One large fat lady was just beaming as He spoke. Over half had left since He started. Then there was a question-and-answer session, and other people left.

Details are vague, but I know that I accompanied Him for two weeks. He didn't always say the same thing. He seemed to tailor what He was saying to the needs of the particular people. Over the course of the two-week period, I noticed that the fat lady was frequently there in the front row. I also began to notice another man—it was hard not to notice him—who had bright red hair and wore a loud plaid jacket and orange pants. He seemed to appear quite frequently. I was concerned that he might be some evil or satanic influence. Finally I said to Jesus, "Master, who is that man?" He replied, "You know— but not at this time," and just smiled. Finally I asked Him why He looked so different. He said, "Of course, everyone would come to see Me if I descended from the clouds in a white robe with angels attending; but that is not My purpose. I'm here to separate the wheat from the chaff. Those who truly know Me will recognize Me in Spirit— the rest will not know Me. In this way I am gathering My true followers." Again I was told by the voice in the dream that the setting of the dream was symbolic—not to be taken literally.—*S.P.*

It's interesting to note that the two figures (other than the dreamer) who remain committed to Christ had physically undesirable qualities—obesity and tasteless dress. A more shallow individual might have rejected them. They contrasted with the "ideal" follower, even as the Christ in the dream contrasts with the "ideal" Jesus-like figure. The whole thrust of the experience seems designed both to test the dreamer's ability to look beyond superficial appearances. It gives the dreamer further reason to suspend judgment on the basis of appearances.

S.P. was told before his experience began that the events were not to be taken literally. The voice encouraged him to go with the flow of the experience, and a letter announced that a Christ encounter was on the agenda. Not all would-be initiates are so fortunate as to have the stage set for them. Especially for dream Christ encounters, witnesses are usually unaware that they are undergoing preliminary tests in preparation for Christ's manifestation. For example, a 42-year-old Catholic housewife believed during one dream that she was participating in a ritual to honor Mary, the mother of Jesus. She was unaware of the initiation process that was under way.

I had a dream that I remembered very clearly and wrote down very soon after awakening. In it, Jesus Christ appeared to me for the very first time.

I dreamed I came across an area that was flat, but out of it came a mound of land that was pyramidal in shape but with a smooth, rounded top.

At the base were many women in long dresses, circling the mound in prayer. They were three deep and encircled the base of the pyramid/mound. I noticed each had a tie on, as if these ties had to be worn by the women in order to be a part of the group. One woman stood out as her tie was of a different sort from the rest. It was hand-sewn, whereas the others looked mass-produced. I thought to myself, "She probably sewed her own tie to join the procession."

I joined the people traveling the base of the mound.

They were praying, and I realized that we were circling a sacred mound—it had spiritual significance.

I remember praying the "Hail Mary." It occurred to me that the mother of God must have appeared on the mound, so that was why the women were praying around it.

As I walked around, I had a feeling that the mother of God would appear. I was fearful. Then, the women circling the mound started to leave. I looked at the top of the mound—I was alone—and I thought I could see a statue of Mary at the top with figures surrounding her. I grew afraid, thinking she might appear. When everyone was gone, three happy women came down—actually floated—from the top of the mound and knelt beside me. We prayed the "Hail Mary." A face I thought could be Mary's appeared. It was only a face, no body. It was of a tired woman—not old but worn by life. I thought, "This must be the mother of God," and I wasn't so frightened but had a feeling of unworthiness. After all, why should she come to see me?

Then I realized there was more to come in the way of visions.

I looked to the sky and saw a figure coming from way in the distance. It grew larger. Much to my amazement and shock, I saw that it was Jesus Christ—a young, handsome Man with a long, white gown and a red flowing cape. He had long hair and a beard, as depicted in popular pictures.

This was a jovial, playful Jesus Christ. He was dancing as He flew through the sky. He reminded me of a combination of Superman and Peter Pan.

I was overwhelmed by the fact that Jesus Christ was appearing before me, for me. It was so overwhelming, I woke myself up.

I don't know what this means. Perhaps . . . the dream

may be pointing out an obstacle I put in my way. Fear,
perhaps.—C.R. (4)

C.R. faced a series of preparatory rituals that involved
overcoming her fear of getting closer to Mary and Christ. Her
fragile sense of belonging was indicated by her observation
that another woman had made her own tie in order to join the
group. Obviously, she felt somewhat awkward and unsure
of herself throughout the dream.

In a letter about her experience, C.R. said that the
preliminary ritual regarding Mary provided her with "a
preparation and support system . . . before He arrived." It
may be that since Catholics hold Mary in the highest of
esteem, C.R. was able to draw upon the spirit of Mary's
willingness and obedience to subdue her own fears before
Christ appeared.

Like C.R.'s experience, the following dream shows us that
most witnesses of the *Initiation* encounter remain unaware of
the significance of the experience until it's almost over. Their
responses to the initiation tests are made without the
reassuring knowledge that Christ awaits them at the end of
the ordeal. The following is a classic *Initiation* encounter. The
dreamer—a 42-year-old female engineer—passes through
several tests of her fearlessness and resolve. Like other
successful initiates, M.W. could have aborted the process at
several points during the unfolding drama. Instead, she
managed to prevail over her fears and the arguments of
people around her.

I dreamt that I was wandering around in the dark,
untroubled and unconcerned where I was, but aware
there were many troubled people around me. I kept
overhearing that there was a terrible storm going on and
to keep away from the ocean. I couldn't believe that.
People tried to tell me their horror stories of their
experiences with the ocean and to warn me to keep

away, but I still wouldn't believe there was anything wrong with the ocean. I decided to go to the sea to check it out for myself. At this point, my parents appeared and my mother said, "Oh, Marcia, you're not really going to do that, are you?" I turned to them and answered, "Yes." Then I softened and said, "There is no reason not to go. Why don't you come with me?" They remained very frightened, clung to each other, and stayed behind with all the other frightened, troubled people.

I walked to where I knew the ocean was and, as I did, the darkness began to lighten up. I felt happier and my spirits rose even more as I approached the sea, although I already felt happy and in good spirits. Instead of coming to the ocean, I found myself in the basement of a lighthouse. There was a Man in His 30s with a beard and shoulder-length hair standing there and facing me as I approached. I knew He was the Lighthouse Keeper. He nodded to me. I would have paid more attention to Him, but I was too busy taking in the surroundings. I didn't think He had my answer, that I could find it myself.

The basement was opened, meaning the lighthouse stood on pillars and there were no walls enclosing the basement. Straight ahead of me, behind the Lighthouse Keeper, was a beautiful white sandy beach which sloped slightly upwards. Beyond that was a glistening calm ocean. The sun shone and the temperature outside the lighthouse was wonderfully warm. I was overwhelmed with the beauty of it all. I was filled with joy. I knew I had been right in believing there was nothing wrong with the ocean.

It was cooler in the basement of the lighthouse because of the shade, but not at all uncomfortable. The Lighthouse Keeper continued to stand there, as if He were waiting to speak with me, but I was eager to explore the lighthouse

first. I sensed that He had all the patience in the world
and would wait forever for me. That thought was
strangely comforting to me.

I turned to the left and walked out to a grated wall
which prevented anyone from falling into the ocean. I
looked down and realized that the ocean was very, very
deep and peaceful. I saw sea gulls flying, sailboats
sailing, and white soft, puffy clouds floating. I smiled as
I watched the waves lap up against the grate where I
stood.

Suddenly, I heard a warning from a very frightened,
panic-stricken, unseen person. "Look out! There's a
huge wave coming at you and it will sweep you away."
I could feel this person's despair. I doubted my
perceptions and did not question why a tidal wave
would hit me when the ocean was so obviously calm
and beautiful. Instinctively, I grabbed onto the grate
wall, crouched down to brace myself, squeezed my eyes
shut, and waited for the wave to hit. Nothing happened.
I was slightly ashamed of my reaction. I understood
immediately that I should have had more faith that the
lighthouse was solid and stood on a very firm foundation.
As I straightened myself up, I forgave myself
immediately for doubting. I thought, "There was no
wave." Then I understood that even if there had been a
wave, there were no waves the lighthouse could not
absorb. The lighthouse stood on solid rock.

I turned around and went back to where I had last
seen the Lighthouse Keeper. (I was ready to meet Him
now.) He was still there, but off to my right. This time I
noticed that His arms were crossed at His waist and that
He cradled a large book in His right arm.

I smiled up at Him. (I'm a tall woman, but He was a
tall Man. I felt like a child in comparison to Him.) I was
so happy. The talk just bubbled out of me. "I don't

understand it. All these people told me not to come here.
It's so beautiful. They don't know what they're missing.
They don't know what they are talking about. Do you
know what just happened? Someone tried to tell me I
was going to be hit by something terrible, but nothing
happened. It's so safe here. Why don't more people
come? You take care of this place, don't You? You're
always here, aren't You? It's always safe here, isn't it?"

"Yes," He replied, "I am always here and it is always
safe." Then He became very gentle as He explained,
"People have to find their own way to Me."

I could not contain the happiness I felt. I wanted to
stay with this Man. I wanted to stay in this place. I felt so
loved. I felt so safe. I would do anything He asked me to
do. I told Him, "I am so glad I came here. I will never
leave You."

With that, He turned to lead me up the path to the
lighthouse door. The path and the door were out in the
sun, off to the left. The door looked black against the
white walls of the lighthouse. I knew He would show
me the inside of the lighthouse once we reached it but,
as I took my first step to follow Him, the dream ended.

There is no doubt in my mind that the Lighthouse
Keeper was Jesus. The first time I wrote down the part
about seeing Him, I kept being overwhelmed with
emotion. Tears of joy were streaming down my face, my
hands shook, and I was forced to keep drying my nose.
Even now, just remembering the dream or reading it
gives me incredible joy and peace . . . Just like the
apostles did, if Jesus appeared again to me and told me
to follow Him, I would drop everything and do it
without a moment's hesitation. I still don't believe I
have begun to capture the emotions I felt in the dream,
but I hope I have given you some sense of what occurred.

—*M.W.-Acct. #1*

Given the culmination of this dream, one can look back on the earlier stages of the experience and appreciate the meaningfulness of the tests that arose. If M.W. had believed the fearful warnings about tidal waves, she might never have arrived at the lighthouse and met the Keeper. There was a plan operating behind the scenes of her dream. The unpleasant situation in the beginning was simply part of a larger design at work. It was an initiation test to see whether she would give in to fear or press onward with faith and courage. Her positive response throughout seemed crucial in determining the outcome of the experience. The eventual encounter with Christ profoundly *reinforced* her faithful, courageous attitude. It's not surprising, therefore, that witnesses of such accounts come away more concerned with their *response* to life's challenges than to the threats they seem to pose.

In the following dream, M.B. moves from victim to initiate. She comes to accept that her own spiritual path might parallel Jesus' own meaningful ordeal.

> I was with Jesus and a group of other people. He was to be crucified. The people and I were walking with Him and trying to keep the crowds away from Him so He wouldn't be hurt. People were trying to be so cruel to Him, throwing rocks and beating Him. We were fighting them off. He was to take up the cross. We took up crosses also. I remember a cross being placed on my shoulders. There was an ugly man there that tried to urinate on me. I kept hitting him. At the end of the dream I went up to Jesus and threw my arms around Him crying, "Do You have to suffer so?" And He said, "Yes, to take away the sins of man." This dream was at the beginning of my realization that the spiritual path was not such an easy one, that we all have crosses to bear.—*M.B.-Acct. #4*

M.B. takes a step toward accepting fully her own path of discipleship. To her, this involves a willingness to see the hardships in her own life as necessary and meaningful. Maybe it seems morbid to take this on willingly, but many individuals report that accepting such an ordeal confers a surprising strength and that each successive trial is surmounted with relative ease.

St. Paul wrote that he "died daily" in his service to the Lord. (I Cor. 15:31) It may not be far from the truth to say that we, too, must be willing to die to fulfill our own initiation tests. But death has many forms, only the final and most literal of which is the demise of the body. Arguably, the sacrifice Christ calls the initiate to make has nothing to do with physical death. Instead, it has to do with relinquishing old ways of thinking and reacting—the ones that prevent us from entering into a closer walk with Him. The *Confrontational* and *Initiation* Christ encounters all seem to point in one direction—toward the need for *a new response* to our familiar, troublesome challenges. It's a response that is essentially what He would do in the same circumstances.

# Chapter Seven

# Spiritual Instruction

From time to time, most of us yearn for greater clarity about our lives. The conventional sources of guidance come with their own biases. Ministers represent God, but may too quickly offer pat religious formulas that coincide with their own all-too-human views. Psychotherapists extol the world of the psyche and the unconscious, but can inadvertently exaggerate the pathological dimensions of our search. And psychics are presumably tapped into records of the soul but often make statements that could with regularity pertain to anyone. Indeed, few persons in our lives seem sufficiently informed to give us what we need: instruction about how to go about living as meaningfully as possible, with a conviction that we are doing what we need to be doing.

The possibility that Christ Himself provides instruction to

individuals is an awesome prospect. Undoubtedly, few of us consider this likely to happen to us. We remain convinced that we'll have to "go it alone," deriving instruction and piecemeal guidance from less lofty sources. In the accounts we examine in this chapter, however, we'll see experiential evidence that Christ may, indeed, provide spiritual instruction to ordinary individuals.

These experiences contain directions about how one should live. Thus, they are potentially the most controversial in the entire collection of accounts. For, if Christ tells one person what he or she should do, then His teaching can be taken as a relevant message for other people as well. After all, one would not expect Christ to change His basic teachings from person to person. Beyond the specifics of His words that are meant for that person alone, His instruction can be taken—rightly or wrongly—as a contemporary revelation of His will for humanity. Because of the potential use to which these accounts can be put, we might do well to consider some of the problems created by these types of reports.

For example, one might well ask, "Are we supposed to accept the validity of the purported instruction *without question*?" If we don't, why not? On whose authority could we depend to validate or invalidate the directives issued by the Christ figure? Another way to approach this issue is to ask, "How can we assess the validity of a Christ encounter outside of the recipient's own subjective feelings?" These are difficult questions. The problem in addressing them may account for why such experiences are largely ignored by religious authorities today.

Certainly, it would be unwise to reject the authenticity of these experiences merely because they conflict with existing doctrines, or even because they contradict the recipient's own personal beliefs. After all, Jesus was always shaking up people. Rather than fitting into what people expected, He boldly defied the expectations of His closest followers and offended virtually every existing system of religious and political authority of His day. The guidance He offered was, in some cases, a ticket to martyrdom. He admonished people to leave their families and wealth in order to follow Him. In many instances, they suffered unfair persecution and eventual death at the hands of the Romans. So we can hardly invalidate contemporary Christ encounters just because they challenge established beliefs and expectations, or ask individuals to carry out difficult tasks.

In fact, the opposite may be closer to the truth. Christ's two simple and bold commandments —(1) to love God and (2) to love one's neighbor as oneself—may forever run somewhat counter to those beliefs which gain easy acceptance. To illustrate: Few Christian spokespersons were willing to join Billy Graham in the mid-1980s in applying Jesus' second commandment to the people of the Soviet Union. It was much more popular—and involved much less risk—to consider that nation the embodiment of evil in the world. Graham was seen by many as a well-meaning pawn of the Communists. But looking back, one can argue that he was divinely led to support a nascent movement toward freedom and spiritual renewal in the long-oppressed Russian people.

Similarly, the apostle Peter's decision to eat at the "unclean" table of the Roman centurion—an action foreshadowed and encouraged by a dream-vision—brought on a storm of controversy at the time because of its deviation from the Jewish law. (See Rom. 10.) Here again, an authentic spiritual initiative went against the grain of popular conventional sentiment. Even when our "neighbors" are so disagreeable as to make the application of Jesus' second commandment appear unreasonable, He apparently meant for this rule to apply to all persons in our lives.

The question of validation can also be addressed through methods that have been used to assess the authenticity of New Testament passages. Today, some New Testament scholars rely on the "principle of dissimilarity"[22] to discriminate between the authentic utterances of Jesus and those passages which may have been altered somewhat by the Gospel writers and translators to cushion the impact of Jesus' unpopular pronouncements. To put it simply, these scholars confer the stamp of authenticity upon a passage to the extent that it *goes against* the popular religious ideas that prevailed at the time. They figure that the Gospel writers were motivated to fit Jesus' teachings into the Jewish prophecies so that Jesus could be seen as the Messiah. Given this aim, they would not have intentionally undermined Christianity's survival by including passages that challenged the prevailing sentiments or religious beliefs of the day—unless they were indeed Jesus' own words. So these unpopular passages, in particular, are more likely to be authentic utterances that the Gospel writers felt duty-bound to include even though the passages stood to provoke and alienate many in that audience.

From this standpoint, contemporary Christ encounters should not be dismissed outright if they contain nondoctrinal teachings. While it is likely that individuals today more readily accept Jesus' teachings than did His contemporaries, it is nonetheless questionable whether Jesus would fit perfectly into any present particular religious system. After all, very few of Jesus' own words have survived to instruct us; and a great deal of modern-day Christianity has been built upon secondary authorities, as well as upon our own questionable abilities to interpret Jesus' own words. If contemporary Christ encounters are what they appear to be—authentic contacts with the Founder of Christianity—then Christ encounters should be seen as possibly containing information which could supplement or clarify the historical words of Jesus. While this might seem heretical, it is a short logical leap to conclude that authentic encounters with Christ might contain information which was not included at all in the brief Gospel record.

# Categories of Instructional Material

This chapter deals specifically with experiences in which Christ offers general instruction and guidance. One can divide the range of possible instructional material in contemporary Christ encounters into three broad categories based on a comparison to the Gospel record:

• Identical to the Gospel record. These utterances are identical or at least equivalent to Jesus' own recorded words. They represent an unequivocal restatement or paraphrasing of His teaching in the Gospels.

• Contradictory to the Gospel record. These teachings specifically contradict Jesus' historical teachings.

• New to the Gospel record. These statements introduce topics never specifically addressed in the New Testament account, thus neither agreeing with nor contradicting His known teachings.

As for the first two categories of instructional material, at face value it seems relatively easy to validate or invalidate a particular Christ encounter on the basis of comparisons that can be made with the Gospels. For instance, one woman—S.L.K., whose account is included further along in this chapter—heard Jesus say that it was all right to divorce her husband after trying for several years to make the marriage work. On the basis of Jesus' words in Matthew and Mark, one might conclude that this Christ encounter cannot be valid, unless her husband was having an affair at the time—the only reason cited by Jesus to justify divorce.

However, before dismissing such an experience, let's remember that all interpersonal communications are open to distortion by the listener. Haven't we all had the unfortunate experience of interpreting someone's statements in a way that was not intended? Presumably, the same error is possible in communications from Christ. With this in mind, it might be possible to preserve a measure of validity to this and other controversial Christ encounters. Certainly, it's possible that

S.L.K. projected her own subjective desires onto the otherwise objective encounter with Christ. She herself wondered at the end of her account: "Where does subjective and objective meet?" Her response was, "All I can say is, 'I know what I know.' "

The third category—that of new teachings—is more difficult to validate. In the absence of any absolute guidelines, we are left having to make personal judgments. We could start by comparing the new teaching with Christ's instructions in the New Testament to see if they seem to bear the same authorship—a quality that can only be assessed subjectively. Beyond that, we could examine the history of Christianity to see if the teaching ever gained a following among well-respected Christians and why it was ultimately rejected by the Church. Those who accept the validity of other religions can compare the teaching with the tenets of Buddhism, Hinduism or another great world religion.

In the final analysis, we are left with having to make a personal decision. For, no one who believes Christ still lives can say—without demonstrating the utmost in presumption and spiritual pride—that Christ has said all He will ever say to humanity.

In the accounts which follow, Christ teaches the recipient an important truth that needs to be acknowledged and applied in his or her life. In most cases, He does not address the practical issues that the recipient faces in everyday life. Instead, He tends to convey instruction of a global nature that the recipient can subsequently apply in a variety of related areas.

In the following account, one woman receives a revelation about the purposefulness of her suffering. At the time, she was 27 and had just come through a series of very difficult situations with her health, career and relationships. But the experience provided instruction to her that wasn't related just to one specific problem but instead was more universal in meaning. Christ taught her about the crucifixion and how it related to her life. By referring to His own tragic death as "positive," He helped her appreciate the meaningfulness of some of her own struggles. Significantly, Christ does not specifically cite the aspects of her life which correspond to her own "cross" but gives her the opportunity to conduct her own life review and to arrive at her own conclusions.

I had a visitation from Jesus on March 6, 1987. It was not a dream. I actually saw Him standing alongside the bed. He was wearing a white robe and a red sheath draped over His shoulder. He had a beard, mustache, and long, light brown hair. His physical appearance was what we humans imagine it to be.

Anyway, while Jesus was by my left side, I was lying on my back with my head propped up and my eyes wide open. We looked at each other and, as I gazed into His clear blue eyes, He said: "L., everything that happened to you, yes, was negative. But, look at it this way."

Jesus extended His left arm out as an indication for me to look in that direction. I turned my head, looked toward His hand, and saw a movie in the air. As I was viewing the movie, I noticed that there were crowds of people along both sides of the road. The crowd from the movie and I (in bed) observed a gentleman who was dressed in shabby red and white garments. He looked physically weak and exhausted as He walked down a road, because He was carrying a wooden cross upon His shoulders and back. Then it dawned on me that I was watching Jesus' own personal story of that very day He changed the world for all humanity.

Right at that moment of understanding, the Jesus alongside my bed asked, "You see what happened to Me?" as His hand extended toward the movie. "Yes," He answered, "it was negative," and His hand reached into the movie. Then, at the very moment He took the cross off His own back in the movie, He said, "But actually, it was positive."

Jesus removed the tiny cross from the movie, turned around, and faced me. However, the cross in Jesus' hand had transformed into a black addition sign about the size of a baseball.

For a few moments, He held the black cross in front of me and then said, "This cross *is* positive."

I looked at the black sign as He continued.

"L., what happened to you was actually positive."

While I looked at Jesus beside me, I thought about the meaning behind both His story in the movie and the black cross He held in His hand. My thoughts quickly reviewed all that I had gone through, and I had received a complete understanding as to why the adverse events happened to me. Even though I had physically and emotionally suffered, these hardships were actually a spiritual gain. These losses were for my soul's growth here on earth. I thought how fortunate I was to experience these negative situations in this lifetime. I was so thankful that Jesus came to me and grateful for His healing, by answering my questions.

When Jesus knew that I was finished with my interpretation of the "Big Picture," He took my left hand and held it in His, saying, "Here, I want you to wear *this* cross." Jesus then placed the black cross into my hand.

I definitely knew that Jesus placed the cross in my hand for I felt two sensations. One, I could feel the weight of the cross (His cross), which was unbearably heavy to hold; and second, the cross was like a hot iron on my palm. My hand was scorched. I had to fan myself from the burning heat. Then Jesus vanished.

Exactly one year later to the date, through a dream I was instructed to look at my left hand. I did so. There in the palm of my hand I saw a red, raised scar of the sign of the cross—the same cross that Jesus placed in my hand upon His visitation. When I awoke from my dream that morning, I looked at my hand, but there was no scar. However, I did trace the lines in my palm and, sure enough, there were two: one horizontal, the other vertical. Today, my palm lines show that there is a cross.

I am greatly honored that Jesus Himself came to me. Sometimes I just wonder. There is not a day that goes by that I don't think of His visitation and what it represents in my life. When I look at my hand, it reminds me of Jesus walking to Calvary and what He said to me that very night: "You see what happened to Me? Yes, it was negative. But actually, it was positive. This cross *is* positive."—*L.B.*

The above account perhaps represents spiritual instruction of the deepest kind; for Jesus takes L.B. beyond a superficial assessment of her suffering into a profound new understanding of her life based on its parallels with *His* suffering and death. Yet He does not offer specific guidance concerning the directions she should take on the basis of that deeper understanding. It is as though the experience is sufficient to awaken in her a response to life that will affect numerous situations.

We might take note of the style by which this spiritual instruction comes. Jesus does two things: He "reframes" her life struggles as positive, and then gives her a chance to review her own ordeal and assign positive value to it. It is interesting that this style of intervention—reframing her circumstances and then allowing her to conduct her own life review—has been incorporated into a contemporary therapeutic approach used by a growing number of modern psychotherapists.

Deriving much of their methodology from the field of

hypnosis, "strategic" therapists will often use language in such a way as to reframe a person's problems so that he/she will begin to see them in a new, more constructive light. In down-to-earth language, we might refer to the constructive recasting of one's problems as "making stepping-stones out of stumbling blocks." Modern-day therapists recognize reframing as a powerful therapeutic intervention all by itself. It literally reconstructs a person's sense of reality and allows for change that was not possible within the limited scope of the old reality. Interestingly, some therapists have recognized Jesus as a strategic therapist *par excellence*. One of the founders of this school, Jay Haley, even wrote a book examining the "power tactics" that Jesus employed as a change agent.[23]

On the heels of successful reframing, strategic therapists will, as the Christ figure did for L.B. in the above account, offer open-ended, somewhat ambiguous suggestions and tasks that are designed to optimize the chances of spontaneously discovering new strengths. Advocates of this strategic method of counseling believe that an open-ended, indirect approach has a double benefit. Not only does it facilitate spontaneous healings and breakthroughs, but it also encourages the patient to discover his or her own resources rather than depending excessively upon an external authority.

I experienced this "therapeutic style" in two Christ encounter dreams which were separated by several years. In both, Jesus spoke to me in symbolic or metaphorical terms about my life, much as He did in His enigmatic parables. These experiences still serve a use as somewhat mysterious and indirect statements against which I compare my current choices and attitudes.

In one, Christ spoke to me about the pearl of great price:

> I am in a dark room. The only thing I can see at first is Jesus standing in front of me. He is discussing the pearl of great price, as though it were an acquisition I should

seek. He is also saying that I must take care not to collect more than one pearl, for then I would be unable to close the lid of the treasure chest that contains it. I see a treasure chest in my mind's eye which is stuffed with pearls and cannot be closed.

I then see C., my fiancée at the time. I conclude that Jesus is talking about life partners and that I should settle on one rather than keep my options open. I say to her, "I guess this means we should be married." I take a sip from a wine glass, then give it to her. It is as though we are consecrating our decision.—*G.S.S.-Acct. #3*

In the parable of the pearl of great price, Jesus likens the pearl to the kingdom of heaven. He tells of a merchant who, upon finding the pearl, is willing to sell everything to have it.

It was understandable that I interpreted Jesus' instruction to me in a very specific way during the course of the dream. While He was probably referring to my need to commit myself to God above all else, I interpreted His words in terms of human relationships. For at the time, I was on the fence regarding my engagement to C. and looking for guidance anywhere it could be found.

I came to see the experience as a reminder of a strong tendency of mine: to preserve too many options at the expense of becoming singularly committed to anything. From my practice in counseling, I have come to realize that many people, especially men, are seriously afflicted with this fear of commitment.

This encounter demonstrates how easily we can look for *specific* guidance from an experience which is only designed to address a *general theme*. No doubt, this is a tendency that many of us have, especially when we're looking for yes-or-no answers to complex questions. It's easy to see why individuals frequently overlook the broader implications of their Christ encounters in favor of an "answer" which satisfies some temporary need.

In a second dream, Jesus spoke to me again concerning the same general problem, again offering spiritual instruction with a metaphorical solution.

> I am with Jesus and His disciples on top of a high hill. He is washing our feet. I am deeply moved and honored by His gesture. When He comes to me, He speaks to me while He is washing my feet. He says that I have a problem with my breathing. He says that I need to learn to breathe in a deeper, different way. Once I learn this, He says, I will not have to breathe as often.
>
> —*G.S.S.-Acct. #4*

Immediately following this dream, I thought that Jesus had been referring literally to my physical breathing. But when I had trouble seeing the validity of that advice, I realized that He was probably addressing my need for deep meditation, i.e., spiritual "breathing," since I had fallen down in my regular meditation practice at the time.

As time went on, the spiritual instruction of this experience seemed even more global. I began to see a link between the themes of the first and second dreams. Eventually I realized that Jesus had again referred to the same problem: a scattered, unfocused outlook. In the previous dream about the pearl of great price, the lesson was to focus and to make a singular commitment. In the second encounter, it was to slow down, to savor my experience with greater depth and quality, and to place less emphasis on quantity. This lesson, I realized, could be applied to breathing, to meditation, to relationships, and to any number of other issues in my life.

One might even object to interpreting these first three events. True, the accounts themselves are rather vague and indirect. But if God had wanted them to be clearer, wouldn't He have just put them into our own language rather than relying on our ability to interpret them? Beyond the reasons already cited, it is likely that the highest truths actually transcend the harsh, either-or nature of language. As mentioned earlier, Carl Jung was one of the first Westerners to recognize that the highest expressions of God within our limited understanding always assume the form of paradoxes, in which two incompatible facts about the Divine are both somehow true.

The following two accounts take this idea a step further and suggest that some instruction may be so subtle, incomprehensible, or inconceivable that it simply cannot be recalled. The recipient—a 65-year-old woman who had the experience when she was 56 years old—was undergoing surgery at the time of this encounter.

> Sometime during my surgery, I was floating very high in dark blue space. I did not have the physical body I have on earth. I chuckled at how small I was. I was all lit up like a tiny light. I had little arms and hands and could see behind me without turning or looking behind. I was delightfully happy. I then floated over the hospital. The surgery room was on the second floor and my hospital room was on the sixth or top floor. I looked down into the surgery room just as though the upper floors were not there. I chuckled again at how small everyone was from my vantage point. I knew that was I on the operating table. Then I thought, "Are you sure?" Just by thinking this, I backed up and went sideways where I could see at a better angle. That was me all right. I then went at a rapid rate of speed back down to the operating table. I was not concerned with anyone or anything except a glowing golden light in the shape of an arc over my head . . . I saw the surgeon and can tell you exactly what he was wearing and what he looked like. However, I had no interest again in what was going

on, as the upper right portion of the room was replaced with the same dark blue space in which I had been floating. In the upper center of the blue space was a tiny white spot or a little white light. This light was getting larger and larger. Then I realized it was approaching at a rapid rate of speed, and it took on the shape of a human. From approximately 15 to 18 feet away the Figure stopped. It was Christ—when you look into those eyes you have no doubt. Without speaking, He communicated a message. I cried several times, "I don't know how. I don't know how." I tried to get up to go to Him but found I was strapped to the table above the waistline by a white two-inch strap. I told Him again, "I don't know how." All of a sudden all the anguish and anxiety left and I was filled with peace—then off to the right appeared crystal-clear mountaintops which seemed to surround a valley that was glowing with light. From this valley came beautiful music, like a whole choir of angels singing a cappella. I continued to hear beautiful classical music right up to the time I woke up in my room the following morning. I immediately told my husband, "I saw God." His remark was, "Well, if you say so."

Later, another encounter occurred in a dream. I woke up remembering that Christ spent the whole night talking to me, giving me important information about something I was supposed to do. But when I woke up, I forgot everything He said! I was so distraught that all day long I begged to dream of Him once more and hear His instructions again so that I could remember them. Well, I awoke the next day with the same exact feeling, and again I had forgotten everything He said. I decided that whatever He said went into my subconscious and perhaps I wasn't ready to hear it yet. The last time I felt His presence was about four years ago during Mass at our church. He was very happy with our congregation and felt a genuine love coming from them. I can only add that each time I feel His presence an undescribable feeling comes over me, and it is always a warm and loving one.—A.R. (2)

A.R.'s experience raises a question: Does the instruction we receive in the Christ encounter need to become a fully conscious realization? Or can this guidance operate just as effectively on an unconscious level, motivating us without our full knowledge of it doing so? In other words, if we forget what He tells us, do we lose the benefit of His guidance? Of course, there is no way to know for sure. But perhaps no matter how much information we remember after such an encounter, it is still unlikely that we could immediately grasp the full implications of His words. We have seen in many other instances how the recipients find themselves pondering the meaning of the Christ encounter for some time before a fuller understanding sets in. If we place exclusive emphasis on conscious understanding, we might miss a great deal as we move too quickly to a final interpretation. Instead, it would perhaps be wise to rely on the capacity of our deeper selves to register and respond to the full meaning of the experience.

Apparently A.R. was told to do something for which she felt unprepared. Again, it is easy to relate to her predicament. Just as many of us are afraid that God would ask us to do something we don't *want* to do, some of us are also afraid that He'll ask us to do something we don't *know how* to do. We can perhaps take heart by remembering just how unwilling and *unprepared* His own disciples were to follow Him—and how so completely they eventually served Him.

It is interesting to see Christ again exhibiting an indirectness and subtlety in the following account which goes to the heart of the dreamer's own neglected sense of humor about the spiritual path. He had been active in the Methodist church while in high school but had drifted away during his college years. In graduate school, his roommate had been a philosophy major and the two of them had many long discussions concerning religion, God, and related issues. During that time he began to meditate and to take spiritual growth very seriously. By his own account, he became overly pious and much too serious. Being religious was important to him, but that seemed to mean giving up fun and frivolous activity. At this time, he had the following dream:

> I was attending class in a large auditorium on campus. The room had a capacity for a hundred or more students and reminded me of the type of classroom where freshman history was taught. I was sitting in the middle of the room and there were only a few empty seats remaining in class. Class had just begun and the lecturer for the day was God. I was listening intently to everything God was saying (although I remembered nothing later), when I heard the rear door to the auditorium open. I thought to myself, "Who could possibly be coming in late to God's class?" When I turned to look, it was Jesus coming down the aisle toward me with a smile on His face. He took a seat one row behind me and three seats to my left. I was totally amazed that Jesus would be late to class and still be smiling. As He sat down, He looked over to me and winked. I turned around quickly and was astounded! I kept saying to myself, "Jesus winked at me! I can't believe it. Jesus actually winked at me!" Then I awoke with an incredible feeling of peace and joy.

As I pondered the meaning of the dream the next morning, I began to realize that being spiritual did not mean maintaining a serious and pious manner, but enjoying the life we are privileged to have while continuing to listen to God's word and practice the lessons He teaches us. The dream was telling me to "lighten up"—even Jesus winks and has a sense of humor. That dream has meant much to me during the past 20 years. Whenever I begin to take my role too seriously, invariably my mind recalls that dream and gently reminds me to "lighten up."—H.C.

Some readers might find Jesus' humor out-of-line with the seriousness He exhibits in the New Testament accounts. Since we know so little about how Jesus lived and interacted with His friends, there is no way to know if He joked and laughed a great deal or maintained a serious attitude throughout His life. Hugh Lynn Cayce—late president of the Association for Research and Enlightenment, Inc., and the son of Edgar Cayce—had several Christ encounters during his lifetime. When he told of them in his many lectures on Christ, he often said that Christ typically exhibited a sense of humor when manifesting to him. Similarly, when his father provided a series of inspiring psychic readings on the life of Christ, he underscored Jesus' sense of humor by saying that He even joked playfully on His walk to Calvary.[24] If this is true, then it is easy to see why Christ would consider it important enough to manifest Himself to a person who had overlooked the role of humor on the path to wholeness.

The following moving account is an emotionally healing encounter that provides guidance to the witness as well. Mentioned earlier as a particularly controversial Christ encounter, the experience nonetheless gave the recipient—a 27-year-old woman at the time—the strength she needed to end her marriage.

Around '79, I was married and still living in Austin, Texas. I had a B.F.A. in art, had worked as an assistant art director in advertising, and had opened a store in a hotel with imports I was bringing in from Hong Kong. I was successful in many ways, but my marriage of six years was failing. I was still spiritually oriented but not particularly "religious." I had been reared in the Catholic religion but saw no particular importance in Christianity other than good ethical dogma on a par with Hinduism or Buddhism. I was going through a period of strife concerning my marriage. I considered my "vow" of marriage very serious but found my current condition intolerable. I felt unsure and guilty at the time to leave my husband, but opted to try to "ride it out."

One morning I awoke and sat up in bed. My then-husband was still sleeping. The room took on an eerie grayish misty glow. Before me in full form appeared the Lord, Jesus Christ. There was no question for me who this was. He spoke to me in words, but not real words— more of a non-verbal, but somehow still verbal communication. He told me to be at peace. He told me it was all right to divorce my then-husband. He bestowed tremendous peace on me. We just loved each other. He told me He would see me again before I died. Then He left. Needless to say, I was awed. I did not even consider myself a good or believing Christian at the time.

I remember laughing that no one would even believe this. Shortly thereafter, I disclosed this experience to a friend of mine who had been a printer for the Maharishi Yogi for several years. He shared his witnessing of supernatural phenomena at times and put me at ease with my experience.

I did proceed with my divorce about one year later. I discussed my experience with Christ to my family and friends, but usually met with ridicule or disbelief.

—S.L.K.


It is probably true that when we feel loved, we are most likely to move off dead-center and take some risks to grow beyond our stagnation. S.L.K. apparently needed to know that she had tried her best and could, with a clear conscience, move on. Today at 41, she is remarried and has two stepchildren.

But many scripturally committed individuals do not believe in divorce except in cases of adultery—the only exception cited by Jesus. So, they would find this account hard to accept, unless the husband's adultery could be established. Advocates of a scripturally consistent position would consider this experience obviously invalid and the Christ figure a clever embodiment of deceit. Exponents of a more liberal view might argue that Christ's teachings today would be somewhat different in order to adjust to the context of contemporary values.

Both of these positions say nothing about what the witness might *contribute to the unfoldment of the experience.* They are focused on the content of the experience, not the witness's own beliefs and biases, which might distort the content somewhat. From this position, one can argue that S.L.K. ultimately *inferred* that Christ approved of her divorce, even though He may have not intended to take any stand at all on the matter. Ultimately perhaps, a case could be made that virtually *all* presumed guidance is generated from within as the recipient reviews his or her choices in Christ's loving presence. If we accept this possibility, then the more controversial guidance can be seen as the product of a self-directed inner search which is activated when one is in His loving presence. From this perspective, the Christ encounter recipient gains access to answers *as* the witness comes into His presence, *as* a consequence of having risen in awareness to a point where the answers naturally proceed from the recipient's own enquiry—not so much *from* Him in an external sense. Now this may seem like splitting hairs. But by locating the source of direction *within* the self as well as in Him, it does two extremely important things: It keeps us honest so we don't try to divorce ourselves from the guidance we receive; and it keeps us in touch with the possibility that when we

come before Him, we are meeting in Him the fullest expression
of our own evolving natures.

The following dream of a 27-year-old man resembles the
earlier dream about the crucifixion. Again the recipient learns
a profound truth about Jesus' death on the cross—that He
lives! Interestingly, the man comes to this realization through
the agency of a mediator—an angel who explains the
significance of what he has witnessed.

> After falling asleep, the following happened:
>
> I was lying in bed. It was morning, so I got up and
> went to the kitchen and sat down at the table. As I looked
> out the window, I saw a cross in the garden with Jesus
> on it. I was really concerned about this and wanted to
> check to see if it was actually He. I was able to look past
> the window and found myself outside (but not with a
> physical body). The air seemed to be in waves, as if the
> air was 2,000 years old and sort of liquidy.
>
> I was able to get very close to Jesus and wanted to
> know if it, the cross, and Jesus were real. I was now right
> beside Him. I could see Him suffering terribly and I felt
> a lot of distress because He was hurting so much. He was
> dirty with blood, and you could smell spit/sweat—not
> repulsive, but just that He had been through a lot of
> abuse.
>
> The problem was that the weight of His body caused
> His arms to be too stretched—because His hands were
> nailed to the cross. As He tried to lift His body up to
> relieve the pain a little, it caused Him even more pain. It
> was really difficult.
>
> I then began to inspect Him, as though through a
> microscope. As I went down over His body, I realized
> He was naked, and how awful that must be for Him to
> be exposed like that—embarrassing. I felt so shocked
> and shameful that I withdrew and found myself back in

the kitchen.

(As this vision was taking place, a dream was also occurring. The dream was that I was waiting for my sister to arrive. Her middle name is Gabriel, and she was living in British Columbia at the time.)

As I sat there wondering what I could do to help, to try to stop the suffering, an angel appeared from above. The angel had no form but was beautiful. The angel told me that he/she had been sent by God to tell me that I, as the Apostle Peter, had been with Jesus when He was on earth. To show me that what had been said was true, I would be turned upside-down—which I was. When I returned right-side up, the angel said I would be able to repeat this whenever I wanted to and left.

(In the dream section, my sister had walked in the front door.)

I began to wonder at this and sat down. I heard a very loud, terrifying scream. I knew that it was over, Jesus had died, and I felt sorrow, guilt, fear. As I thought about these things, the angel reappeared and told me that I shouldn't feel sad and guilty, but rather that I should be glad that Jesus died because by doing so He got rid of sin—sorrow, guilt, fear, doubt. He said that I should be happy. The angel left, and I got up to go to the kitchen door that leads out to the backyard and garden. As I approached the door, I looked out the window.

It really was Jesus! Alive! And really very healthy looking. He said my name, but it wasn't my current name. It was another name, but I knew it was mine. He was smiling. I was *so* joyful to see Him! It was sunny and I heard music, really nice! I felt a lot of joy!

Then I woke up. My whole life changed for the better.

At the time, I had been seeking/praying for several years to know if Jesus and reincarnation were real.

—*P.H.*

In this profound experience, P.H. is blessed with a direct experience of Jesus' death and resurrection. Not only does he witness the horror and humiliation of the Lord's final hours, but he also enjoys the glory of His life resurrected.

As we have observed in other accounts, the appearance of an angel or spokesperson alongside the Christ figure is by no means uncommon. This presence typically serves as an interpreter or as a "bridge" between the recipient's human frame of reference and the divinity of Christ.

Because the above account includes a reference to reincarnation, some readers might reject it out of hand on the basis that it conflicts with current Christian teachings. Since we are not in a position to observe what the fruits of this experience might be in the life of the recipient, we really cannot apply the test advocated by Jeremiah and Jesus for evaluating such experiences independent of their doctrinal implications: by their fruits. Even if the reader accepts the possibility of reincarnation, some will balk at the idea that this man was the disciple Peter: It smacks too much of self-inflation. However, one can also argue that being told that one was once Peter can just as easily have a *humbling* effect. After all, Peter betrayed Jesus on three occasions. What great ego delight can there be in that?

Perhaps the best approach to *Instructional* Christ encounters is to accept that they express profound truths that simply cannot be grasped directly. The various metaphorical dreams cited above obviously had little to do with finding pearls, learning to breathe deeper, or winking more often. Given the obvious metaphorical quality of these experiences, why should one treat the mention of reincarnation any differently? After all, it might be the best way to symbolize a truth that has surfaced in a recurrent fashion in a person's life regardless of how many actual lifetimes that individual has lived. Also, by accepting the possibility that one was once a disciple of Jesus, one can perhaps take on the mantle of modern discipleship in a more intense and meaningful way, while at the same time avoiding the mistakes that the historical disciple made along the way.

An *Instructional* Christ encounter can also be quite brief and to the point, as evidenced by the following account of one woman. In this case, the exact instruction is fully understood during the experience itself.

> Some years ago, before falling asleep one night, I was reciting the Beatitudes, and after the "pure-in-heart" one, I called out (silently to God), "Oh! God, make me pure in heart. I want to be pure in heart." And the Lord in all His glory suddenly stood on my right and took me by the arm (I felt it physically), looked at me silently, and led me down a golden path to a young woman all in white kneeling before what I did not see but *understood* to be the throne of God. (I had been given to know that she was a virgin and represented purity.) Therefore, the interpretation: "If you wish to be 'pure in heart,' pursue and practice purity."—M.B.R.

In another instance, a Christ figure taught a 21-year-old woman about the importance of surrendering the material-based ego identity in order to experience the divine Light. Her experience came while attending a four-week residential seminar on creativity and meditation.

> In July, 1974, I dreamed: I am standing in the dining room at the seminar house. The light of sunset pours in through the window, filling the room with Golden Light. There appears next to me a Man of bronze-colored skin. He does not speak, but I feel immense unconditional love from this Man as the nature of His being. I reach out to touch Him, but immediately know that to make physical contact with Him would shatter the beauty and vibration of this experience. He says to

me, "I go first." This communicates to me through an inner knowing that in order to come into the fullness of my Self in this Golden Light, I must release the little me who identifies with the self-centered, material world and allow the greater "I" to have precedence. As He communicates this telepathically, the Golden Light fills my body from the top of my head downward. I am no longer a dense physical body, but a Light body. I notice especially my hair, which is also infused with Golden Light, and understand the transformation of my thinking which is necessary in this Presence.—*C.N.-Acct. #1*

Fifteen years later, this same woman once again dreamed of a Christ figure who conveyed to her a general teaching that was related to the importance of serving others. Presently she belongs to a small group of women who study the Holy Mother as well as their part in the preparation for the Second Coming. The dream seemed to come in response to their asking the Spirit to instruct them concerning their role in preparing for the Second Coming of Christ.

I dreamed I came to see a concert given by a Christ-like Man who was a singer. He traveled across the country collecting food for the needy and donating both food and concert proceeds to people in the towns in which He sang. He dressed completely in white, owned nothing, and generated the assistance of those who had to give to those who didn't have. He did this by asking the concert-goers to bring food with them as part of their contribution. It was then distributed to the poor in each town He visited. The concert was being held in a large stadium outdoors with tiers of bleachers full to capacity. Everyone attending was dressed in white. When the Singer entered the stadium, everyone rose and there was a visual image of this sea of white rising to greet the Man in respect and reverence. His hair was even silver-white. As the concert began, I became aware that we were all on a train which began to move, taking us all with Him as He sang. The words "Feed my sheep" came to me as I wrote the dream down the next morning. Others in the group had similar dreams of giving out food and a theme of the color white characterizing the dreams.—*C.N.-Acct. #2*

It is easy to see, especially in this woman's second account, how a dream experience can have at least as much impact on the recipient as a waking encounter with a Christ figure. Rather than hearing words directing her to serve others, the dream involved her in an emotionally compelling *experience* of carrying out the teaching itself in a contemporary setting.

We have seen that Christ's instruction is usually very simple. In the following dream, He shows the witness that there is no limit to what he can do—with Christ as his partner:

In my dream, I was riding on a tractor that was pulling a large tiller. I noticed that Jesus was driving the tractor. I was next to Him on the right fender of the tractor. I was talking to Him about my problems and what I was going to do with my life. He looked at me at this time and, before He could speak, the tractor's right tire blew out. Jesus didn't even blink an eye.

I was amazed because we were still plowing. Normally, we should have come to a stop. I asked Jesus how this could be. He answered that there wasn't anything we couldn't do together.

I was still amazed and in disbelief when the left tire blew out. Jesus looked at me again and said, "Oh, you of little faith. Have I not told you that we could do anything together?"

We finished plowing the entire field together on two flat tires.—*M.H. (1)*

This man is a large, powerful individual with a great deal of emotional intensity. The image of the tractor adequately captures the man's own power. But the flat tires reflect his up-and-down struggle with alcohol, drugs and troubled relationships—problems which have afflicted him for many years. Like most deeply spiritual people, he casts a big shadow. Yet Christ seems to say, "That's all right. We can deal with that, *as long as we do it together.*"

In conclusion, we have seen that some individuals receive spiritual instruction in their Christ encounters—teaching that goes far beyond problem-solving for normal day-to-day decisions. In these accounts, we can see how the Christ figure expresses the import of His teaching through metaphor, imagery, and powerful emotional experiences which convey the essence of the teaching. On the one hand, we can breathe a sigh of relief that these teachings restate the enduring truths already familiar to Christianity and other religious systems. But, on the other hand, they are embedded in a context of imagery and feeling that alludes to subtleties beyond the recipient's conscious understanding. Thus, these Christ encounters offer a meaningful, somewhat mysterious springboard for future choices and actions—a life-organizing focus which never loses its relevance nor becomes fully understood.

One might have thought that contemporary Christ encounters would reveal a Christ manifesting Himself to individuals for reasons pertaining primarily to the collective needs of humanity. Given the way Christ allegedly guided the apostles in the days following the crucifixion, one might imagine Christ sending a contemporary Christ encounter recipient into some form of service to humanity, revealing the true impoverished state of human affairs, or announcing some direction that humanity should take to come into alignment with divine purpose. Such collectively oriented experiences could, presumably, elevate the recipient to the status of a divinely commissioned missionary, if not that of a modern-day prophet. If so, Christ encounters would pose a direct challenge to organized religion.

But as the reader has seen, these accounts do not say much about prophecy; nor do they reveal previously hidden spiritual truths. These accounts say much more about the personal relationship of Christ to those who have encountered Him today. Indeed, the Christ encounters that we have received rarely exhibit a focus other than that of the individual witnesses and their close relationships at the time. In almost all of the cases, Christ seems to manifest Himself to communicate above all else the simple fact of his love for the person during a difficult time in that individual's life.

Consequently, while Christ encounters may provide little information that specifically addresses God's perspective on the collective concerns of humanity, they do reveal in detail and heartfelt depth the type of relationship one may apparently enjoy with Christ today.

# Chapter Eight

# Confirmational Experiences

The Christ encounters examined in this book appear to be, most fundamentally, a profound expression of love and acceptance. Yet each affects the witness according to the need at the time. If a person is ill, the experience can exert a physically healing effect or at least alleviate pain and suffering. If a person is emotionally distraught, the Christ encounter can eliminate fear, doubt, depression, and other destructive emotions. If the person has avoided resolving an important obstacle to his or her own growth, the Christ figure can confront the witness with this unfinished business and provide, as well, an opportunity to work through the impasse. When the individual needs instruction or guidance, the

*179*

experience can point the way. In essence, the Christ encounter typically *illuminates* and *compensates* for whatever is out of balance. That is, after bringing problems to light, the Christ figure has an influence that offsets physical, emotional, or spiritual conditions which have gone awry and re-establishes a more healthy balance. But some Christ encounters occur at times when people don't seem to need a corrective intervention. We have already examined one type that seems to come from "out of the blue"—the *Awakening* Christ encounter. In these experiences, Christ seems "merely" to announce His presence as a way to awaken the person to what could become an ongoing relationship with Him.

Another type—and the topic of this chapter—is represented by those accounts in which Christ bestows praise or confirmation upon the person. I have termed these accounts *Confirmational* Christ encounters. In these, Christ's intervention leaves the witness feeling reassured and blessed by His love. He seems to manifest principally to praise the person for work already done or simply to express His approval for the person without direct reference to anything else.

*Awakening* and *Confirmational* Christ encounters appear to differ from the other types, which typically revolve around a problem or a need. Many of the *Awakening* and *Confirmational* witnesses, in contrast, were not experiencing any apparent problems when their Christ encounters happened to them. At least, that is the impression created by their testimonies. Yet, unless one embraces a rather shallow view of happiness, it's likely that few, if any, of us have fully "arrived" even during times of relative stability and contentment. It may be that the *Awakening* and *Confirmational* encounters address a need that *always* exists—to resolve the problem of our own perceived separateness from God.

The fact that such experiences occur at all is significant. They offset the possible impression that Christ encounters occur only during times of crisis. Generally speaking, the other types of accounts reveal a Being who intervenes to point out, correct, or heal imbalances. In contrast, many of the *Awakening* and *Confirmational* accounts reveal a Being who is active and imminent in a person's life during the *good* times as well as the bad.

For instance, the following Christ encounter took place as the witness—an artist—was experiencing a deep sense of meaning about her work. As she feels the positive emotions about her art, Christ appears to her—reinforcing her feelings and her own assessment of her work.

I was busy preparing for a two-person art show that my girlfriend and I had every year. It was April, 1983. I always left everything until the last month. Our show opened in May, so every spare minute between working a full-time job was devoted to the show. I started out with two pastel drawings, very light dreamy drawings called "Dream Roads" and "Transcending." My other pieces were sculpture. I never really planned what I was going to do. Ideas seemed to just come to me.

While I was working on a sculpture in my studio, I was bent over in front of the north window, sawing wood with a handsaw. I felt wonderful. It was then I looked up to the hallway leading into the room. I saw the lower half of a Person in leather sandals and the bottom of a white robe that was so white that it wasn't really solid . . . like bright burning white light. I did not see His face. I looked only from the waist down, and only for a few seconds. I knew it was Jesus. I continued my sawing. The message was loud and clear. I was doing what I was meant to do. I felt very happy.—*R.N.*

R.N. experienced Christ's presence as a powerful confirmation of the path she had already taken in her work.

But she went on to admit that while the sculptures made her immensely happy, they were never a commercial success. This suggests that Christ manifested as a confirmation of her state of mind and heart, awakened by the chosen course of action. But He did not come to guarantee the worldly success of the project itself. To think otherwise might have left her feeling tricked.

Just as Christ seemed to manifest to R.N. to confirm her elevated mood and sense of direction, the following encounter took place as a young girl gradually entered a state of rapture as she sang her favorite hymn. Her emotional and spiritual openness seemed to establish a context in which she could then turn and see what is perhaps always there—Jesus walking beside her.

Ever since my 16th year I've wanted to share an experience which occurred when I was a high school sophomore. I have never shared it with anyone except my mother and best friend, lest someone think I was either lying or hallucinating.

On the maternal side of my family I have Cherokee ancestors; on the other, my grandparents and grand aunt were Shakers. Both Indians and Shakers believe that psychic gifts come from God, and that these gifts include visions and "Dreaming True."

With such a background, it was fairly easy to accept my psychic gifts—until the day I saw Jesus. Although I knew that it was a true and valid experience, I found it both exalting and unsettling.

I was walking the three miles to the place where I caught the school bus in Seddy, Tennessee. Although I can't carry a tune, I was caught up in a sense of at-one-ness with God and began singing "In the Garden" as I trudged along.

As I came to the part of the song in which it says, "And He walks with me and He talks with me, And He tells me I am His own," I sensed a Presence walking beside me on my right. I was in a kind of altered state of consciousness in that moment, a state of spiritual rapture. I have never since felt so exalted, spiritually speaking. As I turned to look, I saw Christ in a three-dimensional form with red-blond hair, blue eyes, and robe of blue. At first I thought He was a "real" person walking beside me.

I was not on any medication and have never hallucinated. The vision was totally impromptu, incited perhaps by the rapture I felt as I sang, off-key, my favorite hymn.—*M.H. (2)-Acct. #1*

Like many of the witnesses of the Christ encounters I've included in this book, M.H. had other encounters in the years which followed. In one memorable lucid dream, she again met Christ face to face.

Forty years later, I had a lucid dream of Christ which seems as real as any event in my life. Today I remember the dream in as much detail and as vividly as I did upon awakening on the night the dream occurred.

The dream began in black and white, but later turned into vivid color.

It started with my being on the edge of a slippery, slimy river bank on a pitch-black night. I couldn't see where I was going, so I crawled along on my hands and knees. Every now and then I would slip over the edge of the bank and down its side, but would catch onto a protruding branch or some other projection, which I could not see. I seemed to know that if, in the darkness, I slid down the black slimy bank into the equally black river, I would be lost forever.

Then, ahead, I saw a white light. I crawled toward it and came to a clearing, a brightly lighted clearing. Now, everything was in brilliant color and beautiful. At the edge of the forest, vividly colored flowers grew. The grass was a bright emerald green.

In the center of the clearing stood a beautiful Southern mansion which gleamed like alabaster. I walked up to the door and knocked, then entered. I was now in a circular-shaped foyer with marble floors. To my right was a circular staircase which led to a mezzanine balcony.

On the balcony stood the Christ I had seen in youth, again wearing a blue robe. He was smiling the same sweet tender smile and held His arms out to welcome me. I felt that I had come home at last.

Remembering the earlier vision and the more recent dream has helped me face three cancer surgeries and four chronic catastrophic illnesses. I shall be in the hospital by the time you receive this for another operation for cancer.

As a result of the God-as-Light dreams, I've written a book-length manuscript of poems about spiritual experiences and have used as the title poem "Walking Toward the Light" . . . —*M.H. (2)-Acct. #2*

M.H.'s lucid dream resembles the kind of perceptually vivid experiences reported by those who presumably gain a glimpse of the afterlife during a near-death experience. While she was not in any kind of physical trauma during the dream, her struggle with chronic illnesses might have brought on this "preview" of her eventual destiny beyond death. Perhaps the earlier part of the dream—her efforts to avoid falling into the river—symbolized not so much her struggle to cling to life but to remain faithfully focused on her eventual destiny—to be with Him again.

The following account also has the earmarks of a near-death experience. But the witness was not, as far as she knew, clinically dead—only recovering from an operation.

At the age of 13, following surgery, as I was coming to,

I found myself held in the arms of a white light Being. I remember feeling very safe and at peace. It felt as if I were a baby being cradled. I turned to look up toward the face and recognized it as Jesus. His robe was brilliant white and He had the warmest, loving smile. No words were spoken but I did not want to leave.

As I felt myself being lowered to the bed (and the pain I knew I'd wake up to), I could see and feel His arms and hands placing me back in my body on the hospital bed. I could hear Him say that it wasn't time for me to stay yet. I could feel His love and wanted to hang on to that feeling forever.

When I woke up and saw my mother, I was excited and asked her if she had seen Him. I was looking toward where I had felt myself come from. I was hoping to still see Him, I guess. No one in the ward had seen anything unusual. My parents always explained it as the drugs from surgery, but to this day I remember the spiritual sight and feel of the experience. (Subsequent surgeries over the years have never brought on any experiences.)

As I read and study, I accept the experience for exactly what it was: a Christ encounter on a plane other than the one we live in daily . . . —S.G.

S.G.'s experience was one of profound love, joy, and comfort. Her relationship with Christ was the only issue at hand—not her beliefs, not her mission in life, not her good deeds, not her sins. Only His love for her. Understandably, this kind of consoling experience leaves many of us focused on Christ's role as Comforter in our lives. But should we seek such consolation? Some think not. In fact, some non-Christian authorities—like American-born guru Da Avabhasa (formerly Da Free John)—criticize conventional Christianity for overemphasizing consolation at the expense of individual responsibility.[25] But it easy to see why the emphasis on the atoning effect of Christ's unconditional love resurfaces with perennial predictability: The experience of His presence validates it.

Even when a confirming experience of His love is imminent, it's not always easy to accept it. In the following account, a young woman experiences a simple but powerfully direct confirmation from Jesus—but only after trying to avoid Him:

> In the dream I was in a classroom lined with benches around the walls, with blackboards at one end . . . Jesus was sleeping on a bench at the back of the classroom, and the feeling was one of anticipating His waking—as the fishermen at sea had—to calm the storm.
>
> As He awakened, I walked toward the door. I was afraid He would look at me, and I felt too unworthy, so I hoped he would not. But He turned and looked at me and came toward me. He then gathered me up to hug me. His appearance then changed to the form of an old East Indian Man, with graying hair cut very short, and a distant twinkle in His eyes.—*R.A.*

R.A. reminds us that it's difficult to feel worthy of Christ's love. If He appeared in our midst today, many of us would probably, as she did, actively avoid Him due to our sense of inadequacy. But notice that He did not wait for R.A. to declare herself worthy: He sought her out. He did not permit her feelings to prevent an encounter. What a statement her experience makes about Christ's willingness to affirm us in spite of our own low self-esteem! Also, it suggests that such encounters may not depend as heavily as we might fear on our own sense of self-worth. The experience itself is a gift—a confirmation of God's love.

There is another interesting feature in her dream, one we've noted in other chapters—that is, the tendency for this Being to assume different forms depending on the individual. It's easy for the mind to get bogged down trying to figure out why a particular personal form manifests to an individual,

why it changes in the course of the encounter, or what form—
if any—represents the "very best" one. Perhaps it changes to
counteract the witness's understandable tendency to place
too much emphasis on His appearance. However, it's also
possible—from the standpoint of reincarnation theory—that
we have experienced, through various lifetimes in other
cultures, other embodiments of Christ consciousness in the
form of gurus and teachers. Regardless of whether
reincarnation is valid, it's still possible that when we "open
the door" to Christ's presence, we also gain access to other
timeless and historical expressions of Him.

Christ's assertion of His relationship with the dreamer
emerges as the single most important aspect of the following
Christ encounter. Again, it doesn't address a problem or
resolve a crisis. Instead, the experience confirms His love for
the person.

Around the summer of 1966, I had a dream about
Christ. Although the contents weren't particularly
unusual, the effect it had on me was profound, and I'll
never forget it.

I was sitting in the balcony of a large auditorium in the
grade school I had attended as a child. I was seated
where I usually sat as a member of the school choir. I
looked down at the stage and saw Christ. He wore a
white toga with His left shoulder bare. There was a large
link chain around His neck, and attached to the chain
was a hank of dark hair about five or six inches square.
The auditorium was crowded, every seat being occupied.
Suddenly everyone was quiet, like a great hush. Christ
then floated upward in a standing position over the
heads of the people below. He floated toward the
balcony—halfway between those of us in the balcony
and those in the audience below. It was very quiet, and
then I heard three beautiful tones of music . . . (I recall
them well as they are the first three notes of an American

Indian chant about a firefly, and one which we sang in
the choir.) After the three tones, Christ spoke, "I am
yours as you are Mine." At that, I was filled with such
overwhelming love and joy, I could never fully describe
it. The feeling was so strong that I awoke.

I felt this way for about three days and could hardly
eat or sleep. At that time, I didn't understand the feelings
because I also felt a sexual love. Until now, I never
mentioned that to anyone as it embarrassed me. I realize
now that if all my [spiritual] centers were stimulated,
this sensuality would probably not be unusual.—*V.B.*

When V.B. shared this moving dream with fellow members
of her meditation study group, they thought that the hank of
hair around Christ's neck signified His mastery over His
physical nature. His levitation above the crowd would be
consistent with this notion, serving as another symbol of His
mastery over the physical realm. This interpretation is
particularly interesting, given V.B.'s experience of intense
feelings of love along with sexual feelings during the
encounter.

Since few persons would argue that sexuality needs to be
obliterated as one develops spiritually, the goal then becomes
to harness it in service of our highest aspirations and ideals.
From this point of view, V.B's sexual feelings *combined with
the experience of Christ's full acceptance of her* could have helped
her to consolidate the union between her human nature and
her spiritual yearnings.

Three of the *Confirmational* Christ encounters we collected
took place in a group setting. The first of these occurred
during a ritual circumcision ceremony for a Jewish infant.
The witness—a 43-year-old Protestant woman—became
aware that Christ manifested to bless the occasion.

The most recent experience I have had with "my
Friend" was while attending a ritual circumcision for

our close friends' first-born boy. The rabbi was circumcising Eric. The ceremony was being held in the dining room. Family and friends were standing all around. My husband, Gene, and I were just outside the door to the dining room, and no one was behind us. The rabbi asked everyone to join in a prayer. My hands were folded, head bowed.

I then realized that Someone was standing behind me. A warmth was at my back. At that point I felt a sensation of a softness of fabric brushing against the backs of my legs. It felt like a long robe. A sense of joy and peace came over me, like a gentle wave. Tears came to my eyes. I smiled. *The Lord was standing right behind me!*

The rabbi was bringing the prayer to a close in Hebrew and English. As the rabbi ended the prayer, I could feel arms being raised behind me, as a blessing was being given to everyone. I looked up at the rabbi. He looked at me with a look in his eyes as though he actually saw the Lord standing behind me. The rabbi then looked down at baby Eric and back at me. I just gently smiled back. It was a soul connection of understanding between the rabbi and me . . . —R.H. (2)

For R.H., the love of family and friends seemed to awaken her to Christ's confirming presence. We do not know what, if anything, the rabbi experienced. He may have seen a Christ figure. More likely, he "only" witnessed in R.H. an awesome degree of love silently expressed through her tears. Through this alone, he may have felt the equivalent of what she experienced. For R.H., it did not seem important to find out for sure what the rabbi experienced, for the bond she felt between them was sufficient for her.

In a similar experience, a woman sees Jesus manifest in the midst of a prayer meeting. Again, only she can see Him.

I was in Tulsa, Oklahoma, at a prayer meeting (in '73 or '74) in the living room of a teacher. There were three rows of people in the living room.

Jesus would first appear to me on the fireplace wall. He was very etheric looking, and I could see right through Him. On one particular night, we asked for a blessing. I saw Him look up and raise His left hand. Then, moving from left to right, He passed His hand over the group. As His hand passed, a tongue of flame appeared on top of everyone's head. The flame appeared in the crown area on the right side of the head. I even felt the flame. Then we started praying for people.

Jesus came down into the center of the group and became as solid and as clear as everyone else who was there. I even saw clearly how His sandals were laced.

He held His arms to welcome everyone. The look on His face was like a mother looking at her newborn child.

The blue of His eyes was like nothing I've ever seen. It was as if the whole eye were blue, a blue that was bluer than the sky.

I asked Him, "Why me? I'm not worthy to be shown You. There are others in this group more worthy than me."

He said, "Why not you?"

I ended the prayer meeting with tears running down my face.—*V.H.*

This dramatic account indicates that no matter how vivid Christ may appear to a person, others may still be unable to perceive His presence. V.H.'s own sense of unimportance tells her that she did not *earn* the experience. Her puzzled questioning reflects this realization. Significantly, Christ doesn't say, "But you *did* deserve it." That would have made His manifestation to V.H. a form of reward. Given what He said, one can conclude that V.H.'s "goodness" or "sinfulness" was not the issue at all. Rather, Christ's love is the issue, and the experience simply confirmed that fact. His elegant and powerful question essentially challenges her—and anyone else for that matter—to present *anything* about herself that could possibly overshadow *His* acceptance of her. The question, "Why not you?" is, perhaps, a succinct statement of His radically inclusive spirit, of His acceptance of each and every person He meets.

Most Christ encounters are reported by single witnesses. Even in the stories of R.H. and V.H.—which took place in group settings—Christ remained invisible to all but one person. In the following *Confirmational* Christ encounter, however, a small group of friends experience an unambiguous sense of His presence as they attempt to re-enact the last hours of Christ's life:

> Our study group tried to re-enact what happened at the Last Supper. We based our activities on an Edgar Cayce psychic reading which gave extensive details about the foods Jesus and His disciples presumably ate during the actual meal, some prayers that might have been said, as well as other details.
>
> We ended the evening with a meditation in which we were apparently visited by the Master Himself! One particular member is very sensitive and recognized His Presence immediately. I myself felt a tremendous vibration and a great Presence of love and comfort, and I could physically feel His strong emanation of power. Others in the group felt something as well, and some simply wept. Soon all of us were crying, and then He actually spoke through our psychic member.
>
> I wish I could remember everything that was said, but what He did that affected me the most was He blessed us, and with that I felt totally humbled and not worthy of such a blessing, yet at the same time I realized how much love He has for me. As I write of this encounter, I

can feel the great vibrations rising within me. I feel I was changed that night and blessed with the ability to be aware of His presence. In the past I might not have been in tune with Him, even though He was there.

In another meditation in our study group, we felt the presence of Mary. Once again, our sensitive group member was present, and I felt another strong vibration and presence, but I *knew* that this was not the Master. However, I felt it was someone equally as powerful. Our group member identified it as Mary, and once again everyone was overcome with emotion and began to weep. She said she came to us because she is attracted to, and has great love for, those who have great faith. One member of our group regularly seeks the Virgin's aid in her prayers, and she was the most moved of us all. I was amazed at how I was able to distinguish the difference between Christ's energy and that of another, and the experience left me with the knowledge that no one could "fool me" and say that they were the Christ.—*C.D.*

We have previously seen that many witnesses report feeling alone in their spirituality following the Christ encounter. Problems are almost sure to arise when one person believes she has witnessed something so utterly beyond the range of almost everyone else's experience. If one keeps it a secret, a feeling of loneliness can prevail. But if the story is told, the witness runs the risk of ridicule and rejection. In contrast, C.D. and her friends were immediately able to share and confirm each other's impressions that something momentous had happened. What a difference sharing the actual experience can make!

Despite the similarities in their experience, it's particularly interesting that each of C.D.'s friends experienced Christ's presence somewhat differently. There are a couple of ways to make sense out of these differences. First, one can accept that the different experiences grew out of the differing legitimate *needs* of each person, and that they were *given* what was particularly suited to each of them at the time.

Another way to make sense out of the differences is to attribute them to the witnesses' differing degrees of *sensitivity* or *openness*. From this standpoint, each person experienced as much as he or she would *allow* into awareness at the time.

It would be easy to say that both explanations are probably valid. But that would gloss over just how different these two interpretations really are. The distinction points to a significant problem in the analysis of Christ encounters in general. We need to be able to tell whether an experience has unfolded as it ideally should or whether it has been limited—or even distorted—by the resistances, beliefs, or expectations of the witnesses. The only way I can think of to answer this question is to solicit more Christ encounters that have been witnessed by more than one person. By looking at how the reports of the same event differ, and then exploring the different beliefs and viewpoints held by the witnesses, one might be able to arrive at a clearer understanding of just how much the witnesses limit and distort the experience.

The group's experience of Mary's presence as a distinct and powerful force of love demonstrates the close relationship often felt between Christ and Mary. In C.R.'s account in Chapter Six, the witness's worship of Mary served as an obvious prelude to Christ's eventual appearance. In A.D.'s account in Chapter Three, the radiant Being was not clearly male or female. We could speculate that Jesus and Mary are distinct beings who cooperate to assist us in our spiritual development and redemption. But we could just as easily say that Jesus and Mary may well be two ways of experiencing the same essentially androgynous Christ Being.

C.D.'s experience above represents the only example of "channeling" that was included in this volume. Yet there are numerous recent examples of individuals serving as the mouthpiece through which higher beings can, presumably, communicate to us. Most of us would probably agree that the quality of a teaching should be based on its merits and not on its packaging. But inevitably, when a "new" phenomenon makes the scene, there's often a grace period in which the method of delivery seems more important than the message itself. In the 1800s, mediumship became the preferred doorway between this world and the next. More recently, psychics like Edgar Cayce have introduced the phenomenon of trance readings, in which a *higher state of consciousness*—rather than a deceased relative—serves as the source of information. As undue fascination with channeling wanes, people will no doubt begin to regard it, too, as just one more avenue by which sacred *and* trivial teachings can make their advent.

C.D.'s account reminds us that Christians have often invoked Christ's presence through ritually enacting significant moments in Jesus' life. From the practice of Holy Communion to the Pope's annual retracing of Jesus' final walk, Christians have historically turned to ritual re-enactment as a way to increase their sense of Christ's abiding presence in their lives.

In a similar vein, many have traveled to the Holy Land and walked the dusty roads that Jesus and His disciples walked over 2,000 years ago. In the following account, a woman sees Jesus walking toward her on the banks of the River Jordan:

> A very special moment with the Master came in 1975 while I was visiting in the Holy Land.
>
> My husband had a dear Jewish friend who lived in Tel Aviv. He arranged for our lodging and planned tours for us when he and his wife were not free to be with us.
>
> On a tour that took us to the Jordan River, I managed to linger behind the tour group. I sat or stood—I cannot remember now—by the river bank. My thoughts were of Jesus and His baptism by John.
>
> Suddenly, I looked up to see the figure of Jesus

walking toward me. Today, I cannot remember what I did or said (or if I spoke). He did not speak, but it was more than a "picturing of Him." Quietly He faded from my vision. I was filled with a renewal of Spirit.

—M.E.-Acct. #3

Once again, so much was conveyed and confirmed in a few silent moments of encountering Christ: His availability, His aliveness, and His love for M.E. About the seeming brevity of such experiences, St. Teresa of Avila once said that "in an instant the mind learns so many things at once that if the imagination and the intellect spend years striving to enumerate them, they could not recall a thousandth part of them."[26]

If we take St. Teresa's words to heart, then brevity is no measure of the significance of a Christ encounter. In the following account, a woman experiences in a few words the awesome power of Christ's confirmation of her:

My vision of Christ came to me in a dream.

I dream quite often about being in a classroom with various teachers, but this time there—standing in front of the class—was Jesus Christ.

He was standing at the blackboard wearing a white robe. His face was not feminine nor physically beautiful as He is sometimes depicted, but His face was kind-looking, a slender face with a dark beard and dark eyes.

He had a kind of glow through His skin. Everyone in the class had a great respect and awe for Him because He was known by all there to be the greatest teacher.

He spoke to the class using such words as "verily." I can't remember His exact words, but He told us that the destruction of the earth had been averted because people had begun to bring forth spiritual energy and send out visualizations for world healing. Then He turned to me and said, "Linda, you are doing better."

When I woke up, I knew that this was not just a dream. It felt as if it had been real. I tried to think about how I was doing better, and then I remembered that a couple of days ago I realized that the most important thing was for me to be loving, and I prayed to be loving. Also, after that, I knew that Christ is really there and I know that I can call on Him and when I do, He comes to me in visions and is always a healing force in my life.

—*L.H. (2)*

L.H. welcomes Christ's approval of her as a great gift and source of information about her progress. But by mentioning that she is only "doing better," Christ also implies that she is still lacking in some way. So, in this encounter we see the teacher-taskmaster side of Christ alongside the comforter-consoler. As such, it's an *Instructional* Christ encounter, too. With full acceptance of L.H., He confirms her. But with full knowledge of her, He also points subtly to work yet to be done.

Obviously, confirmation cannot come to us until we have committed ourselves to some course of action: By definition, confirmation *follows* our choices and actions. A 68-year-old grandmother and grief counselor, who has been married 50 years, began having spiritual experiences about 18 years ago and became worried about her own sanity. After consulting a supportive psychiatrist, she asked for Jesus' help and experienced His presence. He came to her to confirm the spiritual work for which she had been preparing, as related here:

In the 1970s a friend and I were told that together we had some spiritual work to do. We had been studying and meditating for several years but with no particular interest in pursuing psychic experiences. Teachers from spiritual planes began coming regularly and preparing us for this "work." It involved getting our bodies ready to channel very intense energies for the benefit of the planet. Because of this, they said, caution and careful guidance was needed.

Although I have always considered myself a very conservative person and definitely not gullible, there were times when I wondered if I was hallucinating. But I could not, in all honesty, deny that what was happening was real. Fortunately, because I was working closely with another person we were able to reassure each other.

Finally, I consulted a psychiatrist, Dr. Ernest Pecci, a man of much experience in spiritual and psychic matters. He constantly validated my experiences and could not understand why I questioned them so much. But, you see, I really wasn't sure that I should be doing what I was doing. Finally, he said, "Why don't you ask Jesus?"

This seemed very presumptuous and I took no action on the suggestion for some time. However, the need for reassurance became so intense that on May 31 or June 1, 1972, I sat down and asked. A magnificent Being arrived whom I felt certain at that time was Jesus. His presence was immensely comforting and He reassured me that I was doing exactly right.

My impression was that this experience lasted for about 20 minutes. His energy, however, was so powerful, that afterwards I felt completely drained and spent almost three days recovering.

I carried out the assignment for 16 years.—E.M.

It's interesting that E.M. had already set her course but wanted confirmation to make sure she was doing the right thing. As stated previously, confirmation can come only once we've set our minds to do something—after we've analyzed the situation and made the best decision that we can. Edgar Cayce, for one, advised people to do just that: to make a conscious decision *before* seeking confirmation from God.

This suggests a person needs to become willing to be an active partner in the process rather than a passive and helpless recipient. When we underestimate our own capabilities, we skip this step and look too quickly to external sources. It's very difficult for most of us to recognize the importance of forging ahead with our own best decisions. We would prefer that some other willing oracle provide the direction and support that should ideally originate from within ourselves. When we shift away from external approval and enter into the process of our own inner search, our eventual success is often virtually assured.

Perhaps the ultimate confirmation is to be ushered by Him into the realization that we are, as He is, boundless and unlimited beings. The following account was submitted by a 36-year-old woman who, at the time of the experience, was a member of a Christian renunciate and service order. Like many of the witnesses of these encounters, she has had several mystical experiences with Christ.

> I was meditating in the chapel with the other members of the Order. Our collective prayers were to the Master, Jesus, in a spirit of giving ourselves to Him as channels of blessing and service. Then I felt the loving Presence with me and saw white Light pouring into my body and radiating from my face. As I meditated upon this Light and Jesus, I was led interiorly through an encounter like a near-death experience. I passed through a tunnel-like passage into an area of soft blue light, deeper into a dark area, and finally into the midst of a brilliant, shining sun. I remained there in this Light like no other and heard His voice different and separate from the still small voice of my intuition. He said only, "Lo, I am with you always, even unto the end."
>
> I was shown and told a lot from a perspective of a higher knowing but don't remember what was given. What has remained with me is that I experienced myself

as a perfect, whole being with no sense of boundaries or limitations. I was in a complete union and peace with God—there was no separation, not even a concept of being separate—Creator and creation were one in a vibration of infinite Love. I was overwhelmed by the beauty and love that I experienced for myself and all other people at that moment.

In coming out of the meditation, I remember feeling a sense of grief or loss at not being able to maintain the level of conscious awareness and manifestation of that true Self in my everyday life. It was like feeling the atmosphere change when you come down from the high altitudes of a mountain. I wondered why I could not just be that greater "me" all the time. My personality felt like a burden I was carrying around. But I knew that this was the challenge and purpose of my life now—to manifest that awareness and to see others in that Light.

—*C.N.-Acct. #3*

C.N.'s experience of loss as she returned to her "ordinary" state of consciousness underscores one of the dilemmas posed by the Christ encounter: The witness is thereafter consigned to live with the memory of what may never again occur. As Texas-born mystic and author Walter Starcke has said, "It's like having a ten-gallon experience and then returning to a one-quart mind."[27]

The *Confirmational* Christ encounter can resemble a parent-child encounter, in which the parent—beyond requiring anything of the child—simply overflows with love and praise toward the child. A woman experienced silent but profound confirmation as she saw Jesus briefly manifest to her while she was driving.

The first time Jesus appeared to me was when I was driving my car through a city, Cranston, near Rhode Island's capital. He appeared only briefly. I hesitate to

say it was an appearance in the physical sense, but I did
*see* Him. He was sitting in the passenger seat with the
seat belt on! He looked at me, but said nothing. The love
and peace I felt from Him were overpowering. He was
looking at me, not with pride but with pleasure. In other
words, He seemed pleased with me and looked at me
with the type of love a father would have for his child.
—M.W.-Acct. #2

Even though M.W. experienced only love and confirmation
from Jesus, she was still left wondering, "Why me? And what
next?" When she told her minister about the encounter, she
found him supporting the idea that God was calling her. But
to do what? While she admits that she gets scared because she
doesn't feel worthy of this attention, she says that she's "more
afraid of not doing what God wants me to do." She goes on
to say, "It's no exaggeration to say that I am going through
probably the most humbling and exhilarating period of my
life . . . I understand now why the apostles just stopped what
they were doing and followed Christ. If He appears to me
again and tells me to do whatever, I will do it."

It's understandable that M.W. assumed that Christ has
some specific agenda for her. But this assumption runs the
risk of overlooking the most obvious implication of her
encounter—that He manifested to express His pleasure. There
is no evidence that He intended to inaugurate a new course
of action. As already suggested, the Christ encounter
stimulates a search for greater meaning and new directions.
Whether it's His intent that we should be so galvanized as to
pursue a dramatic new course in life is by no means clear
from many of the *Confirmational*-type encounters.

Through the following experience a 52-year-old registered
nurse came to realize that Christ is "*alive now*—in the present."
P.B.'s account is a remarkably luminous and cosmic example
of a *Confirmational* Christ encounter. In addition to portraying

Christ as a Light Being with a sublimely beautiful human side, it includes, as well, the presence of angelic or "spirit guides" who serve as intermediaries between her and the Christ Being.

I am with my spirit guides, Altumus and Miraetha. They are teaching me and giving me a progress report. Altumus smiles at me and says he is pleased with my progress, that I am "becoming." He has never smiled at me before and this is very gratifying to me. They say that I am now ready to meet Someone.

We fly together; Altumus on my right, Miraetha on my left, and I am in the middle. We are flying through clouds, a mist. It is beautiful. Straight ahead, the clouds appear as if the sun is shining behind them, trying to break through.

I can see now that behind the clouds is a very bright white-blue light, sort of like the sun, but not exactly. There are light rays, blue-white, white-blue, shimmering crystalline light rays, streaming above, below, and through the clouds. It is just indescribably beautiful.

The clouds begin to part and the light shines through. It is extremely bright, but does not hurt my eyes. I feel myself being drawn toward the light. It emits something so soothing, so comfortable, so assuring. I am filled inside and out with all these feelings of love, joy, peacefulness, and utmost content.

Moving on toward the light, I see that it is a Being, *it is alive, vibrantly alive!* Without a doubt, this is the *most alive* Being I have ever encountered. He is an absolutely, radiantly beautiful, incredible Being, standing in the midst of the most beautiful, spectacular, shimmering, shining, glowing light which He is emitting. *He is the Light, the Light is He.* As He moves, the light rays radiate His movements. There are NO words. No words exist to describe His beauty and person. *Sublime, He is truly sublime.*

I am close enough now to see His face. I recognize Him. It is Jesus the Christ. *His eyes!* Such compassion! He is looking at me. He knows me inside and out! And it's okay. I feel such compassion, acceptance, warmth, kindness, and understanding coming from Him. There is a radiation of these feelings from Him.

He shows me the Earth, hanging in space. There is something like a halo of shimmering blue, pink, glowing light coming from it. I realize that it is the Earth's aura. The Earth is a living being, too. Looking at it from here, I feel, "No wonder I chose to come here." Wonderful, beautiful, inviting, it beckons me. I feel such a part of it.

Then, He shows me something like a motion picture of the evolution of the Earth, like a movie of the unfolding, the evolvement of the Earth and all life on it. It is progressive, moving, responding to a universal law.

There is a new stage of evolvement beginning now. The Earth is now entering a stage of attunement, at-one-ment. And I understand at once why I am here at this time and why I feel what I feel.

So, that was my dream. On awakening, I was so overwhelmed with feelings that I cried. The meaning, the message was extraordinary. I knew it was more than an ordinary dream, but I didn't know exactly what it was and still don't.

Somehow, in the sleep state, I entered into another dimension of reality, one which was much more real than this one. Christ is alive, He is a living Christ, existing in the present. He is truly present among us and exists with each of us in the "now." Since this dream, I have had a real sense of His presence within me. There still exists that soothing, comfortable, peaceful presence within me that I felt in the dream. It is not as intense, but it is definitely still there and present at all times. Sometimes when I am sad or depressed is when I feel it inside of me the most.

I have an understanding now that my personal wants are not as important. They have taken a lower priority. The most important thing is what He wants for me. So this is my prayer each and every day, that His will be done through me. Some truly amazing things have happened. It is as if I am being guided by unseen hands, led, and always in the directions I need to grow spiritually.

I am an ordinary person; there is nothing special about me. I don't know why I had such a special experience. I feel so humbled and unworthy somehow. Yet the message rings true and clear. I am here for a reason, a purpose, and I must do my part.—*P.B.*

P.B.'s confirming, life-transforming experience anchors her sense of life purpose. The connection comes from a feeling of partnership with Christ. But a relationship with Him can sometimes be a bond that develops *over time.* Surely that was true for a 60-year-old woman who had dedicated her life to searching for spiritual truth from the early age of 8.

I laid down the ideal of my life at age 8: Seek ye first the kingdom of God. For many years I have searched and studied the great teachers. So, when at age 60 I had this vision, I understood it as the culmination of all my previous years' efforts.

While meditating, I suddenly became aware of a magnificent steady sound! It was a high-frequency note that reminded me of Beethoven's "Sounds of the Spheres" and Bach's eternal motion melody.

I looked up and saw the Lord. He was a brilliant white Figure flying from left to right. His arms stretched wide so His garments were His wings. His motion forward made that beautiful sound! On the white garment, every inch of it was covered with human faces. First, I was shocked but quickly understood its symbolic meaning: That the whole universe, humanity included, was the body of Christ!

Later, I encountered Him again. Again as I sat, a beautiful all-silver androgynous Figure appeared. I knew that He was the Lord. Without moving He said:

"I love you till the end of times."

This sentence has become my refuge, my source, and my guide. Such a meeting after 60 years!

I have kept this encounter to myself for many years. You are the second person I share it with.—C.M.

C.M. received the ultimate blessing—a gift of timeless love from the One who is the Source of all her strength and the End of all her searching. It would be wonderful if each of us could know, as she did, that this was His gift to us. It's one thing to accept it on faith, and another thing to hear it, to know it.

Christ bestows this ultimate timeless gift upon another in the following encounters. The witness is again M.L.P.—a woman whose other accounts appear in earlier chapters. Here she points out that her earlier experiences were characterized by Christ appearing to her as all-powerful Master and Healer. In the accounts that follow, however, the relationship changes to a more balanced, reciprocal exchange of love and common goals. As the final experiences presented in this chapter, they reveal a possibility that few of the other accounts directly allude to—that the Christ encounter provides an opportunity to *love Him as He loves us.*

In the dream, I knew that I was on my way to my appointment with Him. I was a child, about 9 years old, and I was glad that I had this special meeting with Him.

The meeting was on the second floor. The stairs were on the outside of the building. I opened the door, walked a few steps down a hallway, and turned into the room on my right.

He was the only light in the room. It was bare. There was no other furniture other than the straight chair He sat on in the center of the room. He was wearing a white robe.

His smile was warm and welcoming, and my heart rushed to Him and urged me to follow. I loved Him so much. But then I realized that this was something I could give Him ... if I didn't take up this time with Him, it would give Him a few minutes to Himself.

He sensed this immediately and was grateful for my gift, knowing what a sacrifice it was to leave Him.

He smiled, a smile filled with gratefulness.

"As long as I live," He started to say and then stopped, knowing that I would misunderstand. He began again, "Wherever I am, I will always remember you."

I backed out of the room and when I reached the hall, I heard soldiers coming up the stairs.

"They're going to crucify Him!" I heard my mind scream and I ran yelling down the hall, down the stairs, past the soldiers, and into consciousness.

This dream was about two years after my first experience.—*M.L.P.-Acct. #4*

There is no way to know whether M.L.P.'s experience was a memory of having known Jesus before or a powerful re-enactment of what it may have been like in the latter days of His life. Of course, there is no way to know. Regardless, the words Jesus spoke to her show us again that His commitment to those who love Him transcends time and death, and sustains us. M.L.P.'s experience also reveals an astounding possibility: that what *we* do and how *we* love somehow sustains Him in return.

Her next two experiences, which took place several years later, also reveal the sense of an evolving partnership.

It was a time in which I was meditating at 2:00 in the morning. However, this experience was in the evening. I was alone in my living room. The evening had a strange quality about it—almost a hushedness. Not spooky, but more expectant. Charged, but in a gentle electricity, not the riveting kind. I was standing, doing nothing, when I heard Him say: "And in a little while, I'll be with you." Nothing more was said, nothing more was needed.—*M.L.P.-Acct. #5*

The last time I saw Jesus was a face-to-face encounter. I remember only this: I was looking Him straight in the eye, person to person. I heard a strength in my voice as I said, almost demanded, not so much asking as requiring: "If I do this, will You be there?"

That was several years ago. I don't know what I agreed to do, but I know that He pledged to be there.
                                                        —*M.L.P.-Acct. #6*

As we review M.L.P.'s Christ encounters, we find that Christ first comes to her bedside and kneels to pray with her (Chapter Two). Soon after, a Being of pure Light heals her physical pain and takes her out of her body to be with Him (Chapter Three). Later, Jesus appears in her car as she voices her concerns about her life (Chapter Four). Then, in the first account above (#4), she rises from the position of mere supplicant to that of being able to give back the love that has been given to her. Then, her final accounts (#5 and #6) point to the pursuit of mutual goals and an eventual reunion with Him.

Our relationship with Christ ideally evolves over time—from an initial act of commitment (which may or may not coincide with an actual encounter) to an equal partnership with Him. This potential sequence depicts our own destiny as, in essence, no less than His own. It presents, at once, an *exalted view* of our importance in the larger scheme of things as well as a *humbling vision* of the awesome responsibilities that stand between us and the greater Home we seek.

# Chapter Nine

# Intimations of His Coming— Forerunner Experiences

So far we've examined numerous examples of Christ encounters. The number of experiences suggests that the Christ encounter is a widespread phenomenon. But we can't avoid the fact that only a few people have been so fortunate. If we take seriously the oft-quoted words of Jesus, "I stand at the door and knock," (Rev. 3:20) then we have to conclude that *what we do* has a bearing on whether we ever meet Him face to face. It also suggests that our lives might be full of *invitations* that we simply fail to acknowledge.

From my own experiences and from some accounts I've received from others, I think it's likely that many of us experience clear indications that a Christ encounter is possible, perhaps even imminent. If so, then most of us probably remain oblivious to these signs. I've named these hints *Forerunner* experiences. They are not Christ encounters per se, but they point to that possibility. Since we solicited only accounts in which witnesses actually perceived Christ's presence, we still know very little about those which might precede Christ encounters. Only a study of the dreams and waking experiences that occur *prior* to these encounters would give us a fully adequate picture of such *Forerunner* experiences.

The most famous recorded Christ encounter of all times seems to contain an allusion to *Forerunner* experiences. When Saul of Tarsus was struck down by his vision of the risen Christ, he asked, "Who art thou?" The Lord replied, "I am Jesus whom thou persecutest: it is hard for thee to kick against the pricks." (Acts 9:5) Some Biblical scholars have pointed to this enigmatic reference, "to kick against the pricks," as a clue. They believe it indicates that Saul had felt Christ's influence in his life *prior* to his conversion experience but had resisted it.[28]

There may be several reasons why individuals overlook these early signs. Perhaps we fear the changes that a Christ encounter might bring and are motivated to overlook the signs of His coming. It might be hard to accept the obvious implication of the *Forerunner* experience—that Someone cares for us and is drawing closer. We are often the last to know when someone else has a special regard for us. *Sometimes it feels just too risky to believe that we're loved.* Consequently, many of us close our eyes to hints of love or to signs of coming good fortune.

It's also true that we often remain unaware of a growth process while we're in the middle of it. Only as we reach the end do we look back and see a meaningful development that has been unfolding all along. As we've all experienced, the graduate is much more likely than the freshman to understand

and respect the learning process. Similarly, it may be hard (although not impossible) to recognize a *Forerunner* experience until after one has had a Christ encounter.

In other words, many individuals who haven't yet witnessed a Christ encounter may nevertheless have had *Forerunner* experiences. Furthermore, these individuals simply haven't reached a vantage point from which they can look back and see the obvious clues in these experiences.

Perhaps those who are interested in experiencing Christ's direct presence could *learn to recognize* the precursors of a Christ encounter in their own lives. Once these indications become evident, they could make conscious efforts to do their part in facilitating an encounter. This recognition combined with prayerful efforts could make the difference in whether *Forerunner* experiences ever give way to a direct encounter with Christ.

## The Types of *Forerunner* Experiences

Upon awakening from sleep, many of us have heard our names called out or heard a knock at the door. Yet when we got up to look, no one was there. Are we being called by Christ? It's hard to know. Or what about physical sensations of energy which seem to announce that something is about to happen to us? As we've seen, several of the witnesses experienced such sensations just prior to their Christ encounters. When we feel tinglings of heightened energy in our bodies, is this the leading edge of a Christ encounter? It's difficult, if not impossible, to know for sure. These inexplicable experiences might point specifically to a Christ encounter, or they might indicate more generally a growing spiritual sensitivity.

I've found that there are three categories of *Forerunner* experiences. In the first type—which could be called "Invitation Experiences"—there is only the subtle hint of His future importance in the person's life. As for myself, the first such experiences happened in church. Twice, as a teenager, I was moved to respond to altar calls, in spite of being there against my will. I might have known that I would eventually turn to Him. But I quickly put these events out of my mind. Later, the invitations came through powerful dreams in which I became aware of a need that could only be fulfilled by Christ, or a problem that couldn't be resolved without His intervention. The potential for actually encountering Christ did not seem to be a part of these experiences. Rather, they *invited me to acknowledge His importance in my life.*

Beyond these subtle intimations, there are clear examples—most of which are probably dreams—of what might be called "Missed Opportunities." In this second category of *Forerunner* experiences, the individual seems headed for a Christ encounter. But somewhere along the way, he or she gets distracted by other interests or priorities and unwittingly loses the chance to encounter Christ. The person's avoidance seems passive or unintended. For instance, on several occasions I've become aware during lucid dreams that an encounter with the Light or Christ Himself would be imminent if only I'd pray and welcome the experience. But so often I've said to myself, "I'll get around to that in just one moment." Instead of immediately assuming a prayerful attitude, I've pursued some interesting sidelight in the dream—and the next thing I've awakened in my bed, kicking myself once again for my imprudent delay.

Third, there are *Forerunner* experiences I call "Aborted Encounters." In these, the witness sees what is coming and *actively* avoids a Christ encounter by reacting with fear, guilt, or other inhibiting emotion. Significantly, this active avoidance indicates that the witness exercises some control over the unfoldment of the encounter, even to the extent that the witness can refuse to experience such an encounter. This ability to refuse to enter His presence points to the cooperative nature of the Christ encounter. It suggests that Christ intends to preserve the integrity of our individual choices rather than to overwhelm our resistances to Him.

Let's look more closely at each of these three categories of *Forerunner* experiences.

## Invitations to a Relationship with Christ

The first type of *Forerunner* experience is very subtle. There is only the hint of an unacknowledged relationship with Christ. But implied is the promise that He could eventually play a more important role in the person's life. For example, before I ever experienced a Christ encounter, I had several dreams which clearly revealed an unacknowledged relationship. Apparently, this relationship existed in spite of the fact I wasn't doing much of anything to foster it. Each dream presented a puzzle or problem, and then pointed to Christ—sometimes subtly and sometimes directly—as the solution to or reconciler of my dilemma.

One such experience happened during my freshman year in college. During that time, several Eastern gurus were introducing their teachings in the U.S. and Europe, and many of their new devotees fervently asserted the need for us all to have a living, physically incarnate master. I had many conversations with my housemates concerning this issue. At one point, I lived in a large rooming house with a follower of Sun Myung Moon, a member of the Baha'i faith, and a follower of Guru Maharaji—the 14-year-old alleged perfect master. They were all interested in convincing me of the rightness of their choices.

One night, after spending an inspiring evening with a friend—who was, at the time, a devotee of Charong Sengh, a Sikh master—I went home wondering if perhaps I, too, should consider seeking initiation from this teacher.

That night I had a dream in which I went to see Charong Sengh in India.

After waiting in line, I was admitted to a small house in which I found him sitting in his turban and robe on a divan. His face was radiant and smiling, seeming to welcome me. But I didn't know what to say! I struggled for words, then told him my name. He nodded and smiled. Then, as I began to ask him a question, I said, "Master . . . ?" He promptly interrupted me and said, "Whose master?!" in a gently admonishing way. With only these words, I realized that he was telling me he was not my master and that I should know that my master was Jesus. A female assistant came out to give me instructions in yoga. As we practiced an asana—the cobra—I experienced an awakening of the kundalini force and saw white light. I looked at Charong Sengh through a white haze and saw that he was laughing joyously.—*G.S.S.-Acct. #5*

It is interesting that Charong Sengh essentially refused my attempt to honor him as master. The surprising twist raised this possibility: A relationship with Christ was preferable to one that I might have with any physically incarnate being. I had not previously considered this possibility. The dream also suggested that this relationship already existed even though I was still largely unaware of it.

I realize that some readers might object to my conclusion that Charong Sengh was referring to Jesus. After all, he didn't specify whom I should serve. Maybe he was referring to the "Master" *within*—that is, my own potential for enlightenment, the potential indicated by the inner Light. But I don't think these two positions are contradictory. Instead, I believe they represent external and internal aspects of the whole truth. To say that Charong Sengh was referring exclusively to Jesus or my own capacity to be like Him is to engage in a fruitless kind of either-or thinking. Ultimately, it would have God residing in one place only.

Around that time, I had another experience which again

pointed to an as-yet undefined and apparently much-needed relationship with Christ. The dream occurred a few days before my 21st birthday. At once promising and disturbing, the dream might be seen as an indication that I would reach a crisis in my spiritual development that only Christ could resolve.

> I am aware that it is time to reveal my life purpose to my parents. So I go to them and invite them to accompany me outdoors into the yard just prior to daybreak. Bearing no physical resemblance to my actual parents, they follow fearfully and hesitantly. I go outside, raise my arms, and begin chanting. As I do, lightning flashes across the sky and builds in intensity. Then I lower my arm and the lightning strikes the earth. This repeats over and over again.
>
> My parents grow so afraid that they pick up a spear and throw it into my back. I realize that I am dying and fall to the ground. They come up to me and look down with horror, regret, and fear in their eyes. I say, "I was really your son. But I am the son of the unborn Son, who is still to come."
>
> I realize that they are shocked to realize that they have killed their son but have not ridded themselves of the problem. I have a sense as the dream ends that they will have to deal with a future son of a more profound nature.—G.S.S.-Acct. #6

The dream dramatized a problem that eventually developed in my life. It's one that afflicts many would-be spiritual seekers: the awakening of deep fears associated with the changes brought on by regular meditation and prayer. Many of us fail to realize that our well-intentioned efforts to become more spiritual actually stir to life powerful unconscious fears and memories. These fears become a "limit to growth," effectively blocking our progress until they can be resolved. This impasse eventually makes it necessary for us to turn to some higher authority for help. For me, I turned to Christ—the "unborn Son" mentioned in that dream years earlier—to heal and reconcile the deep conflicts within me.

These dreams pointed to problems that I needed to resolve before further development in my spiritual and personal life could take place. They provided clear indications that the problems were eminently surmountable through a relationship with Christ. For me there was something ironic about these *Forerunner* experiences: Christ came to represent *both the force of development which awakened these repressed fears in me, as well as the force of love which resolved them.*

The invitations kept coming until I finally accepted a conscious relationship with Him in a dream sometime later. One morning I woke up, feeling irrational fear. I got out of bed and did something unusual for me. I opened the Bible to Jesus' promises to His disciples in John 14-15. Then I went back to sleep and had a dream.

> I am sleeping in a one-room house in which my family lives. I am aware of other family members milling around the room, even while I "sleep." I realize that I am in Palestine at the time of Jesus. As I sleep, I dream that Jesus calls me to leave my family and follow Him. I awaken and tell my parents what has happened. Without regrets, I leave the house on my own and set about to find Him.—*G.S.S.-Acct. #7*

In this final dream of a long sequence of invitational dreams, I found an unanticipated solution to my fears. I found the Way to overcome *all fears*. But it required a willingness to surrender to a relationship with Christ, a relationship that was only slowly dawning in my awareness.

## Missed and Aborted Opportunities

The other two categories of *Forerunner* experiences present an individual with the unambiguous opportunity to commune with Him. In the case of a "Missed Opportunity," the person passively *overlooks* the opportunity by getting distracted by other priorities. In the case of an "Aborted Encounter," the individual actively *avoids* the chance to encounter Him.

Actually, these two types of experiences are probably more similar than they appear on the surface. This is because, in most cases, our tendency to overlook things is motivated by fear and avoidance. I know that my memory tends to fail just before dental appointments, and that I suffer grave lapses of concentration particularly when someone wishes to point out my shortcomings.

So it's understandable that a person might be motivated to ignore or even avoid the obvious indications of an imminent Christ encounter. It can feel overwhelming to anyone who is intent on retaining a firm grip on life. That includes most of us, I'm sure. It's also common to feel unprepared and unworthy for such momentous encounters. For example, guilt over past and recent incidents may come to mind as an immediate reason to disqualify ourselves.

For instance, a woman shared a dream with me several years ago in which she was cleaning her house. She heard someone knocking on the front door and realized it was Christ. At first, she wanted to go answer the door, but then she realized that the house was a mess. So she decided to postpone going to the door and spent the remainder of the dream immersed in housecleaning.

Her efforts to prepare her house before welcoming the ultimate Guest might seem justifiable. Nonetheless, she avoided having an encounter with Christ. Her virtuous sense of propriety was obviously driven by a sense of unworthiness. When are we *ever* ready? If we're going to graduate from *Forerunner* experiences to actual Christ encounters, we have to step beyond our boundaries, even if we don't feel quite ready. The reasons for avoiding Christ encounters often seem justifiable in the context of the dream experience. But all presumably "good" reasons are suspect if they simply justify avoiding a deeply healing, life-changing encounter.

Another way that we can miss a chance for a Christ encounter is by failing to see Him in an unexpected form. I once had a dream that might have provided me an opportunity to encounter Christ. But I believe I walked away from the opportunity. I just couldn't see that Christ might appear to me as a Jew in a three-piece suit.

> I become aware that I am dreaming. I think to myself, "I'm going to look for Jesus!" Excitedly, I begin searching for Him among the people around me. I go up to one man dressed in a three-piece suit. Somehow I know that he is a Jewish man named Joel from New York City. I look closely into his face and say, "You're not Jesus," and turn away.
>
> I never find Jesus. At one point, I stop and ask a man if he's seen Jesus. The old man says, "Jesus doesn't talk to just anyone." I feel that he is referring to me and suddenly feel presumptuous and embarrassed.
>
> —G.S.S. -Acct. #8

Looking back, I realize that I had missed an opportunity to see Christ in the unexpected form of the New York Jewish man. Later in the dream, the old man's words about Jesus' unwillingness to talk to anyone only mirrored my own unfortunate discrimination. The old man could have just as well said, "Jesus doesn't talk to anyone who is not willing to see Him in everyone."

It's easy to fault a person for missing or aborting a Christ encounter. Why would we ever turn down such a precious opportunity? But some people simply aren't prepared when the opportunity presents itself. Taken off guard, they overreact with anxious and fearful surprise.

I am reminded of the joke about the actor who, after having been out of work for some time, got a one-line part in an opening play. His line was, "Hark, the cannons roar!" He went home and practiced for days, saying his line over and over in front of the mirror. On opening night, he went to the theater dressed as a soldier and was instructed to say his part when the cannon fired. The curtain lifted, the cannon roared, and the man yelled, "What was that!?"

Similarly, a client of mine and I were taken by surprise by an overwhelming sense of Christ's presence during one of his counseling sessions. I feel quite sure that we were so surprised and anxious that we limited the experience from unfolding fully. Still, it was an intensely meaningful and uplifting event for both of us.

I mentioned this incident in Chapter One, but I think it would be valuable for the reader to review my client's version of the event.

> I was in counseling with my therapist. I was dealing with many problems, but specifically with drug addiction. My self-esteem was quite low and I was struggling with the split between my spiritual life and my obsessive life of drug addiction. The key thing I remember prior to the experience was that I felt desperately alone.
>
> In the midst of one counseling session, I suddenly stopped talking because I heard and felt a very high-pitched ringing sound in my ears. Then it was as if I, as well as the entire room, had "speeded up"; it was a vibration change—words are inadequate to describe it—but everything around me was intensifying as well. I looked up, and my counselor had a somewhat surprised look on his face. I said, "Something's happening. Is it me?" He said, "No," and there was another intensification in this vibration. "Do you feel it?" I

asked. "Yes," he said.

I felt something like a physical wave wash over me. I could feel the energy flowing over and through me. I remember thinking, "I can feel my spiritual centers opening." I had studied Eastern philosophy and meditation and intellectually knew about the chakras, but in that moment I *felt* them. There was another wave of this energy; it seemed at this point that the whole room was vibrating. My attention was drawn to the corner of the office, and I thought, "It's He," meaning Jesus.

Suddenly I knew what it was like to have Him manifest physically like He did to the apostles after the resurrection. I expected to see Him at any second appear in this corner of the room. I knew He was present, and I was just waiting to see Him. Part of me responded with feelings of unworthiness, such as "I'm not ready," and I believe that is the only reason I did not see Him— because of not feeling worthy of such an experience.

The high-pitched ringing in my ears continued. I still felt a powerful vibration. I still expected, but was afraid, to see Him. The counselor was as tense and as expectant as I. Things slowly began to "quiet" down and I think I said, "Did you experience that, too?"

"Yes," he said. The conversation that followed convinced me that it had been Jesus. The counselor went on to say that he had only experienced that sensation in dreams—and it was usually right before he saw the Light or Jesus.

I felt so grateful and relieved.

My feelings of self-loathing were gone: I had this sense that I was loved more than I would ever know. The fact that I shared this experience with my counselor did not surprise me—for often when we would discuss Jesus I could almost "feel" Him—and I did not feel this with anyone else as keenly as I did with my counselor.

I remembered what He had said, "Where two or more are gathered in My name, there am I in the midst." (Matt. 18:20) I knew I had experienced that in a most literal way. The fact that I shared it with someone validated my experience.—*R.G.*

It might be hard for some people to understand why, after yearning for healing, R.G. and I may have effectively resisted His full manifestation. This understandable attitude, nonetheless, fails to appreciate just how surprising and overwhelming such experiences can be. Everything we claim to be is up for grabs. The control over our own experience slips away as Something else—wondrous and powerful— takes over. What we call reality begins to collapse.

I have found that there is a pivotal moment in the unfoldment of deep mystical experiences in which the individual either surrenders or resists the full culmination of Light and ecstasy. Everything proceeds from this decisive moment, and it is hard to go back and change the course that has already been set. We either enter the Light and meet Him there, or shut the door out of fear and apprehension.

What determines this choice? This "decision" has little to do with the moment itself. Instead, it's a culmination of all we've done up to that point to *define who or what we serve above all else*. If we're clear about this, then surrender becomes possible. For, in that moment of radical and total surrender, we know for sure into whose arms we commit ourselves.

One woman's frightening dream serves as an excellent example of how *Forerunner* experiences can be downright terrifying when we're not sure who is knocking at the door. She was eventually able to see that her fear was unfounded and that it had prevented her from coming face to face with Christ.

Looking back over the 25 years since I became

committed to the spiritual path, I can see that a deep fear of the unknown has often asserted itself at crucial moments when spiritual breakthroughs might have been imminent. For example, I remember spending most of one night during the earliest stages of my spiritual awakening fighting off what I know now was a meditation-induced out-of-body experience. After an especially profound time of prayer and meditation, I spontaneously experienced a sense of flowing out of my body, which was unlike anything I had felt before. My fear of the unknown told me that I was dying, and consequently I used sheer force of will to reject the experience, which offered itself to me repeatedly throughout the night. The opportunity has not been presented to me again.

Several years after that, I had a dream experience in which my deep-seated fear robbed me of the far more precious opportunity to see Jesus face to face. It started out as an ordinary dream, taking place in the office where I worked and involving a conversation with co-workers. Suddenly there was a knocking sound—rap-rap-rap—just like someone knocking on a door. The atmosphere became charged, and I became terrified! Something clearly supernatural was signaled by the knocking, and all I could feel was that irrational, nightmarish fear that is so peculiar to the dream state. I began to pray over and over again, invoking the only name I know to turn to in times of great fear: "In Jesus' name . . . in Jesus' name . . . " As I repeated this simple invocation of Jesus' name, I felt myself catapulted headlong into glorious, radiant light. I tumbled end over end through the light in a spirit of ecstasy, still calling His name.—*L.S.*

L.S.'s immediate assessment of the dream was understandable. She believed that her prayerful call to Jesus had saved her from some horrendous experience. But that was before she came to recognize that her fear of the unknown had always asserted itself whenever she'd been on the threshold of a deeper, inner experience. What struck her was the irony that *it was someone knocking on a door* that so frightened her. Recalling Jesus' words about knocking at the door, she feels quite certain now that if she had responded to the knocking by inviting in the Visitor, she would have met Jesus face to face.

We know from the remainder of Jesus' promise about knocking on the door that once He knocks, we must first recognize Him ("if anyone hear My voice"). Then we must invite Him in ("and open the door") before He will directly commune with us ("I will come in to him, and will sup with him, and he with Me"). (See Rev. 3:20.) As it was, the woman's fear blinded her to His nearness. Instead of inviting Him in, she prayed to Him to protect her from the object of her fear— Himself! He met her on her own terms. Certainly the experience with light that ensued was a reassuring confirmation of His nearness. But, as she says, "I will always wonder what would have happened if I had opened the door and invited Him in."

It's easy to blame oneself for failing to welcome the ultimate Visitor. But some of us simply may not be ready when He first presents Himself. The experience could be a trial run to let us know that more work needs to be done before a direct encounter can take place. So, rather than feeling guilty over having missed a rare chance, we might instead take heart that when we are ready, the Master may again appear. The following story shows us what might have been "behind the door" for one woman. J.L.'s "Aborted Encounter" implies that she may get another chance to meet Him when she feels ready.

> Some friends and I are going to an auditorium to hear a master speak. When we get there, the Master is seated

on a low platform on the stage in the lotus position. He is in a white robe, has long hair and beard, and is surrounded with a white light. He says that His assistants will fill two bowls with water. He will bless the bowls, and then the two assistants will pass between the rows. After the (silver) bowls are blessed, they radiate brilliant white light. The Master explains that as the assistants walk among us, those of us who have the gift will be showered with light and that those people should come and talk to Him (the Master) after the program is over.

The moment He says that, I *know* that another person on the other side of the hall and I will be the only ones singled out. I know that I don't feel as if I'm ready for this experience. As the assistant comes closer and closer, I begin to scrunch down in my seat, trying to become smaller and hoping against hope to be passed over. As he comes into my row, I close my eyes as tight as I can. But when the bowl is held over my head, the light pours over me. It is a physical sensation, like standing in a waterfall or shower of light. Then the assistant passes on. As soon as I recover myself, I rise and leave the auditorium. Once I get home, I am filled with conflicting feelings: the honor of being selected, the fear of the responsibility of such a gift, the guilt for not responding to the call.

When my friends who stayed for the lecture get back, they ask me why I left. I try to tell them I just didn't feel ready and how bad I feel that I was not able to answer this call. They surround me with love and reassurance. They say for me not to worry, that no one had to accept the gift until he or she is ready.—*J.L.*

J.L. said that she did not identify the master as Christ or anyone in particular, "probably because I do not feel worthy of seeing Christ." Even though she avoided the second half of the dream opportunity, she says that she can still close her eyes and feel the sensation of that light pouring over her body.

If we overlook what *might* have happened to L.S. and J.L., their experiences were as fulfilling and complete as many of the accounts in the previous chapters. However, both of these women became aware that they had avoided an experience of a different kind. They had resisted a face-to-face encounter with the embodiment of the Light that so blessed them. Their experiences remain for them fulfilling, but incomplete—forerunners to what may some day become a face-to-face encounter with Him.

# Epilogue

*"Wherefore seeing we also are compassed about with so great a cloud of witnesses, let us lay aside every weight, and the sin which doth so easily beset us, and let us run with patience the race that is set before us, looking unto Jesus, the author and finisher of our faith . . . " (Heb. 12:1-2a)*

It's encouraging to think that many people have already had experiences which point to His coming. Knowing this can give us greater hope that we, too, may eventually enjoy direct encounters with Him. But there is an even more profound possibility that I invite you to consider at this point—that *you have already witnessed a Christ encounter through your empathic response to the experiences of others.*

I saw evidence of this just a few weeks ago. As I was leading my Friday night therapy group, a man told of a Christ encounter that ushered him out of alcoholism into a life of sobriety. He had been a member of the group for six months but had never mentioned the experience that had become the turning point in his life.

He was alone in his apartment, and he came to the stark realization that alcohol had controlled his life since he was 12. He said to himself, "No more." He wandered about the apartment considering all that would have to change in his life. He stopped to look out of a window and saw something shimmering. Then the clear image of Jesus appeared. As he stared at the image, he imagined himself in the back yard of his childhood home, imprisoned in a cage. It was the home where he grew up with a domineering father and an alcoholic mother. As a child, he had been caught between them, seeking futilely to please his judgmental father and trying desperately to heal his mother with his love.

Suddenly in his vision, the bars of the cage lifted, and he was free. This experience became the first step in his difficult journey toward recovery and has since served as a beacon during times of confusion and despair.

The group was transfixed by the man's story. One woman in particular was moved to speak. She first acknowledged that she had never had such an encounter. But then she stated that she now had a clear sense of what it would be like to have something so important and so central in her life—an event to which everything would have to answer. She said she finally realized what people meant when they speak of having an Ideal.

The man's story seemed to have a quickening effect on all of us. I, for one, felt drawn into Christ's presence simply through hearing this man's experience. This event demonstrated to me once again that a *Christ encounter gathers new witnesses through its sharing.*

Having read this book, you have indirectly experienced dozens of Christ encounters, and you have probably been deeply touched by some of them in particular. Like the woman in my Friday night group, we become witnesses to Christ's manifestation through our response to these sacred encounters.

This idea may startle you, especially if you haven't had a direct Christ encounter of your own. You may wonder how your experience of reading these accounts can be compared to meeting Christ face to face.

Think of it this way. Only a few people actually met Jesus during His brief ministry. Of those who did, still fewer understood Him enough to respond to His teachings. Isn't it probably true that His disciples and other true followers—both then and now—are simply those who respond to Him with love and commitment? Doesn't it also make sense that He realized these same followers would tell others about their experiences—thereby expanding His reach into the hearts of men and women everywhere? Indeed, His presence was, and still is, a potent expanding influence that—like the fishes and loaves—multiplies upon contact with others.

So, what does it matter whether this response comes through our own direct encounters or through the experiences of others? When we let go of the need to see Him, we may find that we already know Him through the testimonies of others.

Thus we come together as witnesses. And we meet on a common ground through our common response to the infectious Spirit impelling these experiences.

## A Call to Discipleship?

Each of us must ask, "What do these experiences mean to me? What am I called to do?" These are difficult questions. But the evidence provided by the Christ encounters strongly suggests one answer: Christ manifests to call us into a closer relationship with Him. He seems to expect us to remain in *constant* relationship, or communion, with Him.

But what *kind* of ongoing relationship does He want?

These accounts coincide with the scriptural record in revealing a Master who, in spite of the imperfections in those He chooses, lifts them into *partnership* with Him. It's the same spirit of partnership that called common fishermen to become "fishers of men." It's the same spirit that summoned Paul to become the Apostle to the Gentiles. It's the same spirit that could overlook the betraying nature of Peter and see in him a secure foundation for His church. It's a spirit that calls us to be no less than disciples, even though we remain seriously afflicted by weaknesses and imperfections.

Even if we could bring ourselves to accept the full measure of this invitation, we might still be left wondering what discipleship means *in our everyday lives*. I can only answer this for myself. To me, it simply means living in such close relationship with Him that my every thought and action is considered against the question, *What would He do*? In other words, it means *imitating* Him to the best of my ability so that I can eventually become as He is.

While this might sound presumptuous, I believe it's *all* that He calls us to do. In support of this idea, Christian writer and spokesman C.S. Lewis says that this "is not one among many jobs [that] a Christian has to do; and it is not a sort of special exercise for the top class. It is the whole of Christianity. Christianity offers nothing else at all."

## Potential Pitfalls

Of course, most of us will slip and fall many times before we become full partners and co-creators with Him. What are the likely pitfalls? I can cite three.

*Imposing our own narrow desires.* We can become so confident we are serving Him that we inadvertently cease listening for His promptings: We can begin to take matters into our own hands. Judas exemplifies one who did this by trying to force Jesus to reveal Himself. Apparently, he thought that if he backed Jesus into a corner, He would come out in a blaze of power and glory. He was wrong and saw the disastrous *consequences of his arrogance.* To those of us who are willing to accept a closer relationship with Him, we must resist the tendency to require Christ to come forth according to our narrow desires and wishes.

A dream effectively underscored this flaw in me.

I was back in the time of Jesus, among His close followers. We had been staying in the countryside for some time and did not understand why Jesus was hesitating to go into Jerusalem. We all believed that His entrance into Jerusalem would be the momentous event we had awaited for some time. People would finally proclaim Him for who He was. We were all very impatient to be going.

Finally, Jesus told us that it was time to go. As I left the building where we had been staying, I looked up and saw Jesus looking at me out of an upstairs window. His face showed love but deep sadness. I waved enthusiastically. He smiled at me without saying anything, like a parent who accepts that His child doesn't understand. Then we all took off hurriedly in the direction of Jerusalem. As I awoke, I realized in shock what I had failed to grasp in the dream—that He was going to His death.—*G.S.S.-Acct. #9*

Waiting on His promptings can be difficult as long as we cling to what *we* believe is important. Whenever we try to impose our priorities without regard to His, we run the risk of crucifying the very Spirit we claim to serve. It is a problem that no doubt afflicts many of us from time to time.

My editor and collaborator, Mark, ran into the same sobering flaw in himself. He had just finished a demanding four-day conference, in which he had been one of the guest speakers. As he lay down to take a nap, he felt as if he had really been working hard and effectively for God during the previous days. When he drifted off to sleep, a dream unfolded before he lost consciousness. His full wakefulness carried over into the lucid dream without a break.

He found himself with three other men and immediately recalled that he had met with them every day in his dreams. They formed a group who had a teacher.

As their teacher joined them, Mark saw it was Christ Himself. He began His daily instruction, but Mark's thoughts were already jumping ahead to what he knew would be the culmination of the daily lesson. He remembered that at the end of each lesson, Christ always gave them a "word for the day." This word expressed the essence of what each of them would be challenged to learn during the upcoming day.

Mark felt an extraordinary desire to know that word. It was as if he had had nothing to drink for a day, and the upcoming word was like a glass of water. He was sure his companions felt the same way. Consequently, he was not paying careful attention to what Christ was saying. Instead, Mark was trying to figure out what the word would probably be—as if the new word would logically follow the words they had been assigned before.

Suddenly, he realized that Christ was coming to that part of the lesson where the word would be given. But to his shock and embarrassment, Christ said, "I'm unable to give the word today because one among you is impatient and unable to let go and trust." He named no one, but Mark knew it was obviously he. Upon awakening, he realized that Christ had— lovingly and firmly—held up a magnifying glass to one of his faults.

*Clinging to experiences.* Another problem that confronts us as modern disciples is the tendency to become more attached to the *experience* of His presence than to the spiritual life to which He calls us. This is especially likely for those who have already encountered Him in a direct way. It gives a contemporary meaning to Jesus' words, "Blessed are they that have not seen, and yet have believed." (John 20:29)

It might seem ironic that the experience of His presence could become an obstacle to our serving Him. But anyone who has experienced a Christ encounter can become attached to the awesome gift of His confirming presence. Then, rather than forging ahead on our own, we can come to feel inadequate if we can't recapture that sense of presence. My own experience again serves as a good example.

For several years in my early to mid-twenties, I enjoyed numerous mystical experiences and Christ encounters. But then, as I settled into a stable marriage and career, the experiences slowly diminished in frequency. I missed them, and I wondered if I was doing something wrong. Then I had a revealing dream, which helped me to see the purpose operating behind the decline of my experiences with Him.

> In the dream, I was again with His followers and friends. It seemed that we all knew that soon He would no longer be with us. We were saying goodbye to Him, one by one. I approached Him and embraced Him, sobbing deeply. As I turned to walk away, I saw a man whom I knew to be Peter. We embraced each other, sharing our sense of imminent loss. I was profoundly saddened, but I was also aware that Jesus had told us that His departure was necessary for us to develop more fully on our own.—G.S.S.-Acct. #10

No matter how much we claim to be our own persons, the mere presence of our parents—and other persons of authority—can perpetuate our dependency on them. Eventually, we must strike out on our own before we can mature fully. Similarly, the experience of Christ's abiding presence can, ironically, overshadow our own abilities to become spiritually involved in the lives of those around us. His own words support this idea, when He said, "Greater things than I have done, ye will do." (John 14:12)

*Fear of surrendering.* Finally, I believe there is a third significant impediment to our accepting the mantle of discipleship: our fear of submitting fully to Him. We think we can keep something back for ourselves. We want to strike a bargain in which He gets what He wants *and* we get what we want. C.S. Lewis compares this attitude to that of an honest man paying his taxes. "He pays them all right, but he does hope that there be enough left over for him to live on."[29] This does not seem to be what Christ has in mind. The Christian way, Lewis contends, is much harder and much easier. "Christ says, 'Give me all.' "[30] Something in us doesn't like this idea. We tremble at the thought of turning over our lives.

The other morning as I awoke, I heard a voice clearly say to me, "Now is the time for Me to lay down My cross, and for you to carry it." In reflection, I believe that the cross signifies to me the exquisite burden of surrendering completely to a life of serving Christ.

Further, I believe that my whole life—and perhaps yours, too—comes down to a single question:

Will you?

So, Christ can awaken us to a relationship with Him. As the great Physician, He can heal our bodies and our hearts. As Taskmaster, He can confront and initiate us, encouraging us to remove obstacles to a closer relationship with Him. As the consummate Teacher, He can instruct and guide us into areas of new growth. As the Bridegroom, He can come to reassure us that we are, above all else, *loved.*

Out of this process eventually comes the realization that *He is alive,* that we are called by a living Master to do more than we've ever imagined: to become His partners and to accept the mantle of discipleship; to imitate Him and to grow into a likeness of Him.

Short of our full arrival, it might mean falling into error. It might mean imposing our own selfish desires for a season. It might mean walking alone for long periods without the experience of His consoling presence. And it might mean finally facing our fears of letting go.

As we run this race that is set before us, may we always look to Him. May we all keep the faith that just as He has come to us before, He may surely come to us again.

# FOOTNOTES

1. *Christ Consciousness.* Vol. 11 of the Edgar Cayce Library Series. Virginia Beach: A.R.E. Press, 1980.

2. Fulop-Miller, R. *The Saints That Moved the World.* New York: Thomas Crowell, 1945.

3. Bucke, R.M. *Cosmic Consciousness: A Study in the Evolution of the Human Mind.* New York: Dutton, 1967, ca. 1900.

4. Kirshna, G. *The Biological Basis of Religion and Genius.* New York: Harper and Row, 1972.

5. Sparrow, G.S. *Lucid Dreaming—Dawning of the Clear Light.* Virginia Beach: A.R.E. Press, 1976.

6. Moody, R. *Life After Life.* St. Simons Island, Ga.: Mockingbird, 1975.

7. Morton, R.T. *Knowing Jesus.* Philadelphia: Westminster, 1974.

8. Daily, S. *Love Can Open Prison Doors.* San Gabriel: Willing Press, 1938.

9. Supplement to reading 281-13 of the Edgar Cayce readings. This letter from Cayce was attached to the thirteenth reading in a series given to a group of Cayce's friends who had devoted themselves to serving as channels of healing through prayer and meditation. Most of Cayce's discourses were given to individuals, so that the first number of the reading—281 in this case—would usually represent an individual. In this case, however, it represents the healing prayer group.

10. Ritchie, G.C., with Sherrill, E. *Return from Tomorrow.* Waco: Chosen, 1978.

11. Griffin, W. *Clive Staples Lewis—A Dramatic Life.* San Francisco: Harper and Row, 1986.

12. Fulop-Miller, R. *Op. cit.*

13. Fielding, H. *Tom Jones*. New York: Random House, 1950.

14. Kelsey, M.T. *God, Dreams, and Revelation*. Minneapolis: Augsburg, 1974.

15. Chadwick, H. *The Early Church*. New York: Dorset, 1986.

16. Evans, R. *Dialogue with C.G. Jung*. New York: Praeger, 1981.

17. Rogers, C.R. *On Becoming a Person*. Boston: Houghton Mifflin, 1961.

18. Peck, M.S. *The Road Less Traveled: A New Psychology of Love, Traditional Values, and Spiritual Growth*. New York: Simon and Schuster, 1978.

19. Underhill, E. *Mysticism*. New York: NAL, 1974.

20. Evans-Wentz, W.Y. *Tibet's Great Yogi Milarepa: A Biography from the Tibetan*. London: Oxford University, 1928.

21. Evans, S. *The High History of the Holy Graal*. Cambridge: James Clark, 1969.

22. Hamilton, E. *Witness to the Truth*. New York: Norton, 1948.

23. Haley, J. *The Power Tactics of Jesus Christ and Other Essays*. Out of print.

24. *Jesus the Pattern*. Vol. 10 of the Edgar Cayce Library Series. Virginia Beach: A.R.E. Press, 1980. Also see readings 2448-2, 2571-1, 2984-1, 2995-1, 3003-1, and 3685-1.

25. Lovananda, Da. "The Heart-Breaking Truth." From a lecture delivered to his followers.

26. Teresa, Saint. *The Interior Castle*. Garden City: Doubleday, 1961.

27. Starcke, W. Personal communication, 1972.

28. Stevens, G.B. *The Pauline Theology*. New York: Charles Scribner's Sons, 1911.

29. Lewis, C.S. *Mere Christianity*. New York: Macmillan, 1972, ca. 1943.

30. Lewis, C.S. *Ibid*.

# What Is A.R.E.®?

The Association for Research and Enlightenment, Inc. (A.R.E.), is the international headquarters for the work of Edgar Cayce (1877-1945), who is considered the best-documented psychic of the twentieth century. Founded in 1931, the A.R.E. consists of a community of people from all walks of life and spiritual traditions, who have found meaningful and life-transformative insights from the readings of Edgar Cayce.

Although A.R.E. headquarters is located in Virginia Beach, Virginia—where visitors are always welcome—the A.R.E. community is a global network of individuals who offer conferences, educational activities, and fellowship around the world. People of every age are invited to participate in programs that focus on such topics as holistic health, dreams, reincarnation, ESP, the power of the mind, meditation, and personal spirituality.

In addition to study groups and various activities, the A.R.E. offers membership benefits and services, a bimonthly magazine, a newsletter, extracts from the Cayce readings, conferences, international tours, a massage school curriculum, an impressive volunteer network, a retreat-type camp for children and adults, and A.R.E. contacts around the world. A.R.E. also maintains an affiliation with Atlantic University, which offers a master's degree program in Transpersonal Studies.

For additional information about A.R.E. activities hosted near you, please contact:

A.R.E.
67th St. and Atlantic Ave.
P.O. Box 595
Virginia Beach, VA 23451-0595
(804) 428-3588

# A.R.E. Press

A.R.E. Press is a publisher and distributor of books, audiotapes, and videos that offer guidance for a more fulfilling life. Our products are based on, or are compatible with, the concepts in the psychic readings of Edgar Cayce.

We especially seek to create products which carry forward the inspirational story of individuals who have made practical application of the Cayce legacy.

For a free catalog, please write to A.R.E. Press at the address below or call toll free 1-800-723-1112. For any other information, please call 804-428-3588, extension 220.

> **A.R.E. Press**
> **P.O. Box 656**
> **68th Street and Atlantic Avenue**
> **Virginia Beach, VA 23451-0656**